MASTER BUILDER
RESPAWNED

TRIUMPH
BOOKS

Raid

Swiftness

×4 Fire Aspect

WELCOME TO MINECRAFT EARTH!

So fresh, so clean! Experience Minecraft in a whole new light! Collect tappables, create on buildplates, and build with friends!

LET'S PLAY!

This book is available in quantity at special discounts for your group or organization. For further information, contact:

Triumph Books LLC
814 North Franklin Street
Chicago, Illinois 60610
Phone: (312) 337-0747
www.triumphbooks.com

Printed in U.S.A.
ISBN: 978-1-62937-805-3

Interior design: Patricia Frey
Cover design: Jonathan Hahn

Contents

Introduction

In the decade since its original release, Minecraft has turned into a true cultural phenomenon. Walk the aisles at any department store and you'll probably find shelves of licensed merchandise – and see plenty of kids in Creeper shirts along the way. While players are united by their love for the game, the reasons why they're attracted to it are as diverse as its fanbase. Some are drawn to the thrill of exploring a new world and leaving their mark on untamed lands. Others dive deep into redstone engineering, creating stunningly complex contraptions. And still others just like riding pigs around until the square sun sets. To each their own.

Whatever your reasons, you're in good hands here. A lot has happened in Minecraft over the past few years, thanks to Mojang's insistence on keeping Minecraft fresh by adding new features, gameplay systems, and mechanics. If you haven't played the game for a while, there's a very real possibility that

you'll find yourself overwhelmed with all the new stuff. That's where we come in.

In these pages, we'll do our best to give Minecrafters the solid foundation they'll need to have the best possible time. If you're new to the world of Minecraft, welcome. We'll introduce you to the essential elements you need to know before you set off into the world for glory and fame – hopefully minimizing your failures along the way. Experienced Minecrafters will find some new ideas and tips as well, particularly those who have taken a bit of a break from the game. If you already know what you like to do most, we'll show you how to get there fast. And maybe we'll introduce you to some of your soon-to-be favorite activities, too.

Minecraft is more than just the core title, too. Mojang is releasing two new Minecraft-oriented experiences, and we'll get you acquainted with those. Minecraft Earth is an augmented-reality game that turns your mobile device into a Minecraft portal, like an even more awesome Pokémon Go. Minecraft Dungeons gives combat fans more to look forward to, in an all-new action adventure with loot, bosses, and tons of dangerous mobs to slay.

As big as Minecraft is now, it's only getting bigger. Let's get going, shall we?

The State of the Game

Minecraft is one of those rare games that virtually everyone knows a bit about, whether or not they've spent a second swinging a pixelated pickaxe. Since the original release in 2009, more than 176 million copies of the game have been sold worldwide, making it the best-selling video game of all time. And those downloads and retail copies aren't lying dormant; according to Microsoft and Mojang, more than 112 million players are actively building and exploring every month.

It's remained a powerhouse both as a game and a cultural touchstone, but its recent 10-year anniversary brought it back into the spotlight even further, if that's at all possible. Popular YouTubers who started their careers with Minecraft Let's Plays have returned to the game in a big way, making it seem more relevant than ever. It managed to reclaim the title of most-viewed game from previous titleholder Fortnite, which is a sign of just how strong that renewed wave of enthusiasm has been.

Mojang has steadily updated the game over the decade, adding now-ubiquitous features like enchanting, villages, and rideable horses. Development has also gotten more streamlined, while simultaneously getting a little more complicated. If you're interested in getting into Minecraft for the first time, chances are you're going to face a fairly significant choice right out of the game: What version should you get?

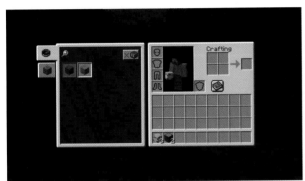 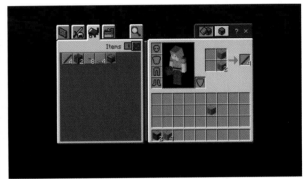

Java (left) and Bedrock (right) have subtle, but important differences, including the crafting interfaces.

If you play on mobile or most consoles, the choice is essentially made for you. PC players have a couple of different options, each with their own positives and negatives. Years ago, the mobile version of the game was available in a form called Minecraft: Pocket Edition, while the PC and consoles like Xbox 360, Nintendo Wii U, and PlayStation 3 had their own versions of Minecraft. Microsoft and Mojang eventually shifted its focus onto building what they called the Bedrock Edition of the game, which provided a unified version that's now what you'll play on the Xbox One, Nintendo Switch, and PlayStation 4. PC players can also choose to play the Java version, which is the original release. Unlike Bedrock, which has been coded in the C++ programming language, Java edition is built using – you guessed it – Java.

Bedrock Edition

Bedrock is in some ways the flagship version of Minecraft. It offers cross-platform play, meaning that if you have that version, you can play along with your friends that have Bedrock, regardless of whether they're playing on a mobile device, console, or PC. It runs better, too, with the ability to render larger chunks of the in-game world without taking a significant performance hit. Playing with friends and adding new content is a smoother experience overall, with a user interface that may be easier for new players to navigate. If you're someone who prefers using a controller over mouse and keyboard on PC, Bedrock supports that without having to add any third-party mods.

One of the fun things that's currently a Java exclusive is the ability to generate Amplified biomes, which essentially turn the terrain up to 11.

Java Edition

Java isn't without its own advantages, however. Updates historically hit Java first, making it a clear destination for people who want to experience the leading edge of what's coming to Minecraft. The modding scene is also much larger on Java, and there are an abundance of multiplayer servers to explore, including minigames that you can only play on Java. There are a ton of other things, both large and small. Some block variations are only available on Java, and the crafting interface is different. You

can pick items up with fishing rods in Java. Most notably, redstone works a bit differently between versions, which can create confusion for players who watch YouTube tutorials and find that they're unable to get things working in Bedrock, since the majority of streamers use the Java version.

Neither one is objectively "better," but there are differences that players need to be aware of. In this book, we'll do our best to provide information that's useful and relevant for everyone, regardless of whether you're playing on Java or Bedrock. In the

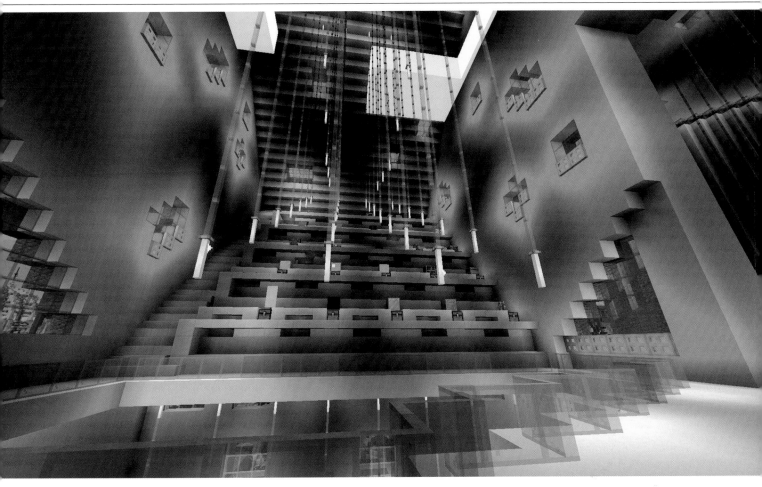

To mark its 10-year anniversary, Mojang commissioned a special interactive museum that highlights Minecraft milestones.

times where a feature is only aimed at one version, we'll be sure to call that out. Keep in mind, however, that Mojang is constantly updating Minecraft, so there's a distinct possibility that features will shift and align between those two versions more closely in the future. In the meantime, let's put on some armor, sharpen those axes, and head out. And watch your step; those Creepers can be a bit touchy.

Biomes

Minecraft's world may be built out of blocks, but don't let the visual simplicity fool you. It's a rich and interesting place to explore, filled with a wide variety of terrain, resources, and, of course, hazards. That kind of diversity can be overwhelming at times, particularly if you're just dropping into a new game. Is a forest a good place to build a new camp? Should you bother heading down that hill to explore the mesa in the distance? Are those … pandas?!

Over the following pages, we're going to take a deep dive into some of Minecraft's most interesting biomes. They're not all great places to settle down in, but most of them have something worthwhile to offer players, provided you know where to look.

First things first: You're going to read or hear the word "biome" a lot if you spend time with Minecraft. Don't feel bad if it's an unfamiliar term. Scientifically, it's essentially a way to group communities of plants and animals together, based upon their common habitat. Minecraft uses the word to describe a specific type of region in the game, which includes the terrain, climate, and types of lifeforms that can spawn in that area. In other words, places like deserts, forests, and savannas are all considered biomes.

If you're playing on Java edition, identifying biomes is trivially easy: Simply press F3 on your keyboard to pull up a debug menu, which includes the type of biome that you're currently inhabiting. Bedrock users will have to learn to identify these environments by sight. Don't worry; even though there are dozens of different types (including many subtle variations that we're not going to go into detail here), once you start to pick up the distinctive elements of the major biomes you'll be set.

There's No Place Like Home: Temperate / Lush Biomes

These temperate locales have a little of something for everyone

Plains

Look no further if you're seeking a great place to start your Minecraft experience. Plains are a fantastic location to establish a home base, thanks to their flat topography and reliably close proximity to natural resources. We can't offer any guarantees, but odds are that you'll be within walking distance to a forest, mountain, river, or other great spot.

Items of Note: Keep an eye out for horses, donkeys, and villages. Finding a village in the early game can be a tremendous boost, thanks to the free shelter, food, and treasure it can provide. If you don't see one, punch down some oak trees and start your own.

Forest

You can't do much without wood, and what do you know – wood literally grows on trees in this biome. It can be tempting to plant your own roots in this area, but be careful: Trees create shade, which can allow monsters to spawn when you least expect it. Even if you're prepared for battle, forest fires can easily spread.

Items of Note: Oak and birch trees are the biggest hauls here.

River

These winding bodies of water can be found all over the place, making them one of the most common sights in the game. They're a great source of water and a perfect place for setting up a starter farm, particularly if you find one bordering a plain. You'll need to pull your own oars if you want to go boating, since rivers don't have currents in Minecraft.

Items of Note: In addition to the water, you can find sand, clay, and sugar cane in rivers, as well as salmon and squid. They can also be homes for the drowned, so keep the vicinity well-lit unless you want to risk getting hit by a deadly trident.

Dark Forest

The name may refer to its abundance of dark oak – one of the only places you'll find the material in the game – but also nails this biome's gloomy atmosphere. The trees here are so thick that even getting around can be dangerous. Add to that the very real danger of daytime monster spawns, and you have several compelling reasons to make this one of the places you'll probably only want to visit, and only then once you're equipped for combat. On the other hand, its dense canopy makes it a fine place for a treehouse.

Items of Note: As we mentioned, this is a prime place for dark oak. You'll also be able to find giant mushrooms and rose bushes. Keep an eye out for woodland mansions, but be prepared for a fight if you head inside.

Swamp

In some ways, this is like a wetter version of the plains. The generally flat arrangement makes it easy to spot enemies, provided you don't have vine-covered trees in your line of sight. Those trees are a distinctive feature of this biome, but they're just oak in disguise. It might look like a hazy bummer, but it's actually not a bad place to spend some time.

Items of Note: Witches like to inhabit swamps, so watch out for their huts and keep a distance. If you don't feel like hanging around these potion slinging creeps, grab some lily pads, fossils, clay, and salmon before heading out. Bedrock players can find giant mushrooms here, too.

Jungle

Here, you'll find some truly massive trees, including some with 2x2 trunks that seem to reach to the clouds. The jungle is functionally similar to a dark forest, so stay out of the shade, unless you're looking for a fight.

Items of Note: Jungle temples can be found here, appropriately enough. You can also spy friendly parrots and slightly shyer ocelots. Melons, cocoa pods, and bamboo grow in this lush area. If you're playing on Bedrock, you can find some frolicking pandas as well.

Bamboo Jungle

Once again, it's all in the name. The bamboo jungle's most noteworthy feature is the plant that gives it its name. Bamboo is all over the place, growing in tall clusters that are impossible to miss. If you're one of those players who thinks sugar cane is bamboo, one stop in a bamboo jungle should set you straight; it's difficult to overstate just how tall these things can grow.

Items of Note: We're not the only ones impressed by all this bamboo. These jungles are also home to pandas, who subsist on the fast-growing treats. Other than that, it's basically the jungle, part II.

Mushroom Fields

This biome is one of the rarer places around, so consider yourself lucky if you stumble upon one. Mushroom fields are typically small islands, with huge mushrooms, small mushrooms, and an earthy surface made from mushroom parts. It's remarkable in that hostile mobs can't spawn here, even in dark areas such as caves. It's unlikely you'll spawn in a mushroom field, but consider yourself safe if you do. That is, until it's time to eat. You can't grow anything on the mycelium surface, so be prepared to haul dirt over if you want to farm or break the surface blocks and hoe it as fast as you possibly can.

Items of Note: We saved the best for last: This area is home to the mooshroom mobs, colorful cows that have mushrooms growing on their backs. You can milk them like ordinary cattle, so if you bring a bucket, you can drink mushroom stew for free.

Chill Out Zones: Cold Biomes

Get ready for rugged adventures and plenty of climbing in these wooded wonderlands

Mountains

Mountains are another incredibly common sight in Minecraft; it seems like you can't pan around the horizon without seeing at least one in the distance. They're home to a wide variety of wondrous formations, including waterfalls, caves, and awe-inspiring (and occasionally gravity-defying) rock formations. If you spend much time around them, you'll want to be on notice for sudden drops and other treacherous terrain. Building your own cave can be a great starting strategy, especially if there aren't many other resources around – provided it doesn't lead to whatever's making that sound in the depths...

Items of Note: If you're lucky, you can find emeralds in the upper reaches of mountains. They're one of the game's rarest resources, however, so don't feel too badly if you come up short. You can console yourself with lumber (oak and spruce), and possibly even an encounter with a llama.

Taiga

You like spruce trees? You're in luck. The taiga is positively overflowing with 'em, especially if you stumble upon the giant-tree variation. These titans have 2x2 block trunks, with straight shots into the sky. The big ones can be easily harvested if you chop them into a staircase-style pattern as you ascend.

Items of Note: Closer to the forest floor, you'll find wolves, rabbits, and foxes, as well as sweet-berry bushes and ferns. Villagers can call this region home, so it's worth getting up high and taking a look around before you move on.

Cool Places to Explore: Snowy Biomes

These biomes don't offer many resources, but the views can be spectacular

Snowy Tundra

If you spawn in the tundra, you may want to get ready to start walking. This biome is fairly desolate, making it one that's not for the faint of heart. You might find an occasional spruce or oak tree, but they're a rare sight. There's a reason igloos can spawn here naturally; ice is one of the few building materials around.

Items of Note: Believe it or not, villagers can inhabit this region, giving you a nice place to recharge before you head out to more bountiful prospects. You can also spy polar bears in this biome, along with wolves and foxes.

Ice Spikes

This is a rare variant of the snowy tundra, and it manages to be even more inhospitable. It's worth seeking this biome out at least once in your Minecraft career, however, since these sky-high shards of ice are one of the most impressive sights the game has to offer.

Items of Note: Look up, and then move along. Take a screenshot before you go, though.

Hot Properties: Dry / Warm Biomes

You can expect extreme conditions and a wide array of experiences in these toasty warm places

Desert

These biomes are typically pretty flat, giving you a chance to spy monsters before they even see you coming. Deserts can be a pleasant place to retire, but you'll want to bring building resources along with you or prepare to move into an established villager settlement. Sand isn't the best construction material, as little pigs know, and that's the most abundant material around.

Items of Note: Sand, sand, and more sand. Also, you'll find cacti, sandstone, and sugar cane. Rabbits make their home here, as do the Husk monsters. Pyramids might be a tempting loot location, but beware of traps.

Savanna

The acacia trees cut a striking silhouette in another one of Minecraft's most visually distinctive locations. These biomes can be found near deserts, and they offer a wonderful respite from those harsh conditions. You'll find plenty of resources here, along with signs of wildlife and civilization. It's definitely another solid starting point for those lucky enough to spawn in this region.

Items of Note: This biome is great if you want to establish a herd. You'll find horses, cows, sheep, and llamas here, and plenty of acacia (and oak) to build a barn.

Badlands

The badlands are yet another rare biome, and they're worth a visit. These colorful canyons are a lonesome place – passive mobs don't spawn – but are beautiful, nonetheless. An eroded variation is even more impressive, featuring tall monument-like spires that jut into the air. It might not be the best place to set up a permanent homestead, but it's worth camping under the stars and square moon for a night or two. If only there were wolves to sing you to sleep.

Items of Note: There's gold in them thar hills! For real! This is one of the only places you'll find gold ore in plain sight, and you can also spot above-ground mineshafts. There are six different colors of naturally occurring terracotta to gather.

Time for the Brine: Ocean Biomes

Explorers who can master the seas may also reap big rewards

Ocean

The Aquatic Update gave the oceans a much-needed refresh. With an abundance of life and colorful sights, there's now a reason to dive under the water's surface. There are loads of different variants, including deeper versions and several temperatures, but the oceans generally share the same overall qualities. It's wet, dark, and often dangerous for those who don't come equipped to hold their breath longer or fight the Drowned who defend these depths.

Items of Note: You might not know it, but there's a lot going on beneath the surface. Dolphins, pufferfish, squid, tropical fish, and turtles make their home under the sea, as do less friendly creatures like Drowned and Guardians. Keep an eye out for shipwrecks, underwater ruins, and ocean monuments. They're worth exploring.

Deep Frozen Ocean

This is probably the most unusual ocean variation, which is why we're calling it out. It looks pretty crazy from the surface, and if you dive under the surface you'll find even more massive icebergs and other weird formations. It's worth holding your breath for these undersea vistas.

Items of Note: As you might expect, you'll find ice and blue ice here, as well as clay and sand. You'll also possibly run into polar bears and salmon, as well as some of those nasty Drowned.

The Nether

Minecraft's hidden world is more interesting than ever

This is one of the go-to destinations for Minecraft players, since it's an integral part of "beating" the game. After constructing an obsidian portal and activating it with a flint and steel, players come face to face with a hellish nightmare: The Nether. This place is not meant for mortal men and women, but that hasn't stopped players from plundering it for the past decade. Mojang recently gave this area a much-needed refresh, with a variety of new sub-biomes to explore.

The Crimson Forest biome is home to the new Piglin and Hoglin mobs. Piglins will leave you alone if you're wearing gold, and if you give them a gold ingot they'll trade with you! Otherwise, these greedy mobs are hostile. Hoglins, on the other hand, will attack just about everything they see.

The Warped Forest is home to Endermen, so watch out. Souls and Valley biomes are a great place to find fossils, but it can be dangerous to explore. The Basalt Delta is treacherous terrain, with plenty of stony spires that make navigation tricky. Be sure to pack ladders if you plan on making a trip to this region. The old Nether is still there, but it's now known as the Nether Wastes.

Items of Note: OK, deep breath. You want building materials? We've got nettherrack, glowstone, soul sand, nether quartz, and magma blocks. You want to fight? How do you feel about taking on Ghasts, Blazes, Zombie Pigmen, Wither Skeletons, and Magma Cubes? Lava also flows like water here, which reminds us: Don't bother bringing water, since it evaporates instantly in the oppressive heat. And woe to the player who tries to bring a bed into this cursed location. Those who try to catch a little sleep will find themselves facing an explosive nightmare.

Striders are passive lava dwellers that can be ridden if you put a saddle on them and use a warp fungus on a stick to lead them around. Lava doesn't bother them, which makes for a safe (but nerve-wracking) ride.

Finally, the Nether update added a new class of gear to the game: Netherite. Mine Ancient Debris deep within the Nether and refine it in a furnace to get Netherite Scrap. Craft four Netherite Scrap with four gold ingots to get a Netherite ingot. Use that at a smithing table to upgrade your diamond armor and tools to the most powerful material in the game: Netherite. It's not easy, but well worth the effort.

Animals, Food, and Farming

Mining and crafting get a lot of attention, but there are other foundational layers to the Minecraft experience. In this section we'll explore several elements of the game that might not immediately seem as though they belong together, but they all feed into one of the largest and most important gameplay loops.

Chapter 4: Animals, Food, and Farming

Cows run wild in Minecraft. Not sure where they are? Follow the mooing!

Every Minecraft world is a complex ecosystem with interrelated elements. If you were to remove one of these things, the whole experience would likely suffer. Fortunately for us, that's not going to happen. For instance, seeds can be planted to grow wheat. That wheat can be given to cows to encourage them to enter what Mojang calls, in the interest of remaining family friendly, "love mode." Calves grow up to be cows, which can be milked or slaughtered for food and leather. You see what we mean?

You've undoubtedly noticed that Minecraft's worlds are populated with all kinds of plants and critters. Some are useful, while others are currently there to add atmosphere or are just for fun. Over the next few pages, we'll break down what you should know – including info on some new creatures that have a significant effect on this aspect of the game. Read on for a deeper look at Minecraft's farming, animals, and food.

Farming

Your first few moments in a new Minecraft world are filled with desperation. Are there any trees nearby? What kind of threats are in the immediate vicinity? Is the sun starting to go down already? Foraging is the name of the early game, and you're largely living a hand-to-mouth existence. Your first goal should be to build or seek shelter, but what should you do next? The answer is fairly clear, particularly if you're playing on survival mode: Set up a farm.

Don't worry; you don't need to apply for any licenses or learn how to drive a tractor. Farming in Minecraft is as easy as planting some seeds or setting down saplings. If the soil and other conditions are met, all you'll need then is a little patience. There's a difference between doing something and doing it efficiently, however. Let's start with wheat, which is probably one of the earliest crops you'll be able to grow. In addition to be easily accessible, it's a valuable way to get across some of Minecraft's fundamental farming rules.

First, you'll need seeds to grow wheat. Oddly enough, you'll be able to get them by destroying grass. Not all grass clusters will produce seeds, so you might have to be persistent. Once you have seeds, you have to create suitable places to plant them. Craft a hoe, and then use it on grass or dirt blocks to till the soil. Here's the thing, though: You can plant seeds on any-old dirt or grass if you're

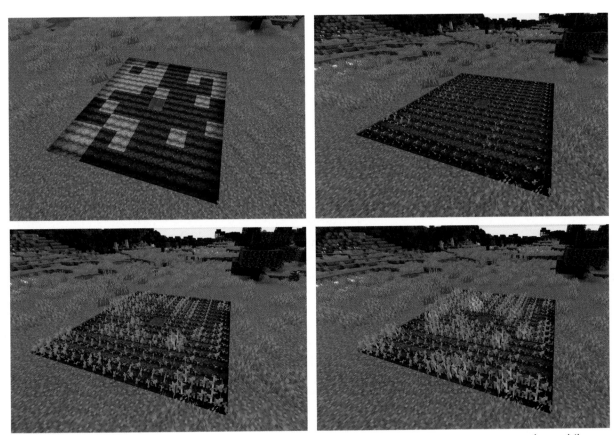

Soil will get irrigated and crops will grow in a random-looking sequence. Be patient, since it may take a while.

fast enough, but if the soil isn't within four blocks of a water source, the wheat will grow quite slowly. You'll want to find a shoreline in the early moments of the game, until you can craft a bucket to place a water source in your field.

There are a couple of different ways you can lay out your farm. You can plant your fields in long rows, or you can cover the entirety of the field. The advantage of leaving space between rows is time; if crops have empty blocks beside them, they'll grow more quickly. Denser planting will grow slower, but also yield more once it's harvest time because there isn't any unused space. The choice is up to you. Once the seeds are planted in appropriate soil, all you need to do is wait (bone meal can speed up the process). After a while, the wheat will grow tall and

turn golden brown. Punch it to harvest the wheat, and pick up any seeds that might drop.

Wheat is a nice starter crop, but there are far better things to farm once you're established. Unfortunately, finding these seeds is slightly trickier. Potatoes, beetroot, and carrots can be found in villages or chests. Once you have these seeds, growing them is similar to wheat. Plant them in tilled soil and then wait. You'll know they're ready when you can see the veggie peeking up near the bottom of the stem. They're guaranteed to drop more seeds, so with a little patience you'll be able to grow as large a farm as you'd like.

As you can see here, bamboo can tower over the similar-looking sugar cane.

Melons and pumpkins are a little different, in that they need a little room to flourish – two blocks, to be exact. Once planted, their seeds will produce vines and then eventually fruit. Don't bother using bone meal on these guys to encourage faster growth, since it won't work.

Sugar cane has long been mistaken for bamboo, which was made a bit more confusing with the introduction of, well, bamboo. These tall green plants look similar, but the process of growing them is slightly different. Bamboo is pretty low-maintenance stuff. Put it on grass, sand, or gravel – no tilling required. After a few minutes, it'll start reaching for the sky. It's a fast-growing plant, and it can reach heights of up to 16 blocks. Sugar cane, on the other hand, has more specific needs. Most notably, it needs to be directly next to water. Once that condition is met, it'll grow up to four blocks high. Both bamboo and sugar cane can be repeatedly harvested, so long as you leave a one-block-high part of the plant. Cut that, and you'll have to replant it. Otherwise, it's almost like giving the plant a haircut. Over time it will grow, and you can trim it periodically. That property makes it a great candidate for automated piston farming, which we'll get into a little later in the book.

Animals

As we mentioned before, there are lots of animals and other creatures wandering around in Minecraft. Some are friendly, some aren't. Most of them offer some kind of benefit or interaction to the player – whether it's offering a food source, companionship, or even just entertainment. Here's a quick rundown of some of the most important creatures in Minecraft's menagerie.

Bees

Type: Neutral

Bees are among the newest members of Minecraft's animal kingdom. They're a welcome addition, thanks to their helpfulness in regard to farming. Just like real bees, these insect workers love plants and flowers. They'll move from their hives (which can be found naturally in oak and birch trees) in search of flowers. If they pollinate a flower, they'll emanate particles and you'll see little spots of it on their backs. Once they've got pollen, there's a chance they'll help out with your farming; when they fly over crops, they can speed up their growth. Afterward, they'll return to their nest or hive for a few minutes and add some honey to their home.

To get honeycomb, use shears on the hive or nest. You can also get honey by using an empty bottle on the hive. Either way, it's a good idea to place a campfire underneath their home first, or else you're likely to get stung by a swarm of angry bees. Angry bees will attack with their stingers, causing poison damage. They'll automatically die after stinging. As with all neutral mobs, they won't attack you unless you hit them first. You don't get any experience for killing bees, so it's probably best to leave them alone and enjoy the benefits of their hard work.

Bees can be encouraged to follow you and also enter love mode with flowers.

Cows

Type: Passive

Cows are a staple of Minecraft, providing some critically important materials. If you want milk, leather, and steak, you're going to want some cows. Cows are peaceful mobs, which means that they'll simply run away when attacked – they won't try to bite back. While they'll need to be alive if you want to milk them (by using a bucket), you'll have to kill them to harvest the other materials. It's the Minecraft circle of life and all that. If you're a little squeamish about doing the deed yourself, we'll show you how to build something that automates the process a little later on.

Fortunately, getting more cows is trivially easy. They'll follow you around if you're holding wheat. Give them the plant, and they'll be ready to have a calf, provided there's another love-mode-ready candidate nearby. A variant, mooshrooms, appear in mushroom fields biomes. These weird critters can be turned into normal cows by using shears to remove the mushrooms that grow on their backs.

Sheep

Type: Passive

Sheep are another common animal that are worth having around your homestead. Killing them will yield some raw mutton. You can use shears on an adult sheep to clip its coat, getting some wool for your trouble. Shorn sheep will regrow their coats automatically, as long as they're able to munch on a little grass. You can take advantage of that process by building an automated sheep-shearing station – and what do you know, we show that off a little later, too.

Just like cows, sheep are really into wheat. They'll follow you around when you're holding it, and feeding it to them will put them into love mode.

Pigs

Type: Passive

Pigs are the final members of our farm-mammal trio, and while you can't milk or shear them, they do have something special about them: You can ride 'em. After finding a saddle in a chest, you can use it on a pig to turn the porker into a means of transportation. You'll have to use a carrot on a stick item to encourage them to go, however. They're not as road ready as horses, but they're a fun way to get around in the world. They drop pork chops when they're killed, which might be a bit of a consolation if you end up accidentally riding off a cliff.

Pigs aren't choosy when it comes to eating. They can be encouraged to enter love mode with carrots, potatoes, or beetroots.

Chickens

Type: Passive

Chickens are another common critter that you'll find strutting and hopping all over the place. They're also versatile creatures, which makes their presence welcome – if you can get past all the squawking. Just like real chickens, they'll wander around and lay eggs. The eggs can be used as food, or, when thrown, can also randomly spawn chicks. When killed, chickens will drop a raw chicken and possibly some feathers. Both of those items are handy to have around, and the egg-spawning mechanic makes them another great candidate for automated harvesting. Keep reading to learn more on that.

Chickens are crazy about seeds, and they'll follow you or enter love-mode if you have some on hand. Melon seeds, pumpkin seeds, wheat seeds, beetroot seeds – it doesn't matter!

Horses, Donkeys, and Llamas

Type: Passive/Neutral

These three guys are so similar that we're grouping them together, even though there are a few critical differences. Horses and donkeys can be ridden, but you'll have to do a bit of work first. Before you can gallop around at high speeds, they need to be tamed. How do you tame them? By approaching them slowly and attempting to ride them. We'll say "attempt," because you're probably going to get bucked off several times before it's used to having a person on its back. Once it no longer attempts to buck you off (and shows some hearts), you can place a saddle on its back and ride it at will. If you have a chest in your hand and "use" it, the donkey will become a true beast of burden, hauling around your gear and saving you some much-needed inventory space. Horses lack that functionality, but they can be outfitted with armor to mitigate damage. Horses and donkeys can be fed golden apples or golden carrots to get them into love mode. If you breed a horse and a donkey, you'll get a mule! These creatures are a lot like donkeys, and they can be equipped with chests.

Llamas are similar to donkeys and mules, in that they can haul your items around, but there are fundamental distinctions worth noting. You tame them the same way you do horses, donkeys, and mules, but you don't need to saddle them to ride. Unfortunately, you can't direct them when you get on their backs. You're basically going to go wherever they want to go. That doesn't mean they're not useful, however. If you use a lead on them, other llamas will notice you're walking with their friend and they'll form a caravan. Tame several, and you can put chests on each one – essentially giving you a ton of inventory space for long-distance journeys. They're neutral, so don't be surprised when they start spitting at you when you attack them. It doesn't do a ton of damage,

but yuck. When killed, they'll drop leather, just like horses, donkeys, and mules. Why attack them, though? In fact, why not make more? To do so, give them hay bales, and they'll enter love mode.

Those are the most important and useful animals, but they're far from the only ones in Minecraft. Here's a quick rundown of the rest of the mobs you might run into, with a few of their most interesting characteristics.

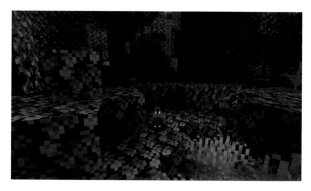

Cats

Type: Passive

Cats spawn in villages, and can be tamed (and bred) with fish. They're shy, so approach slowly. You can tell it's tamed when a collar appears around its neck, just like wolves. If you lead one to your bed and sleep, there's a chance they'll leave you a present. Killing them (monster!) will get you some string, perhaps a reference to the catgut that was once used to make strings for musical instruments.

Parrots

Type: Passive

These rare birds are among Minecraft's flashiest creatures. They come in a wide array of colors, and can be tamed by feeding them seeds. Once they've gotten used to you, they'll perch on your shoulder. They're a must-have accessory for any budding pirate, though finding one can be tricky. They drop feathers when they die.

Wolves

Type: Neutral

Give this doggo a bone! Give him enough, and he'll be tamed and follow you around. Tamed wolves will pitch in during battle, attacking enemies and dealing a little bit of damage. Interact with your pet to have him sit, in case you don't want him to rush into harm's way.

Pandas

Type: Passive/Neutral

Pandas live in bamboo forests, and they're easily one of the cutest parts in the game. There are several varieties, and they're all passive – with the exception of the aggressive ones, which can be recognized by their angry eyebrows. They love bamboo, which can be used to encourage them to go into love mode. Babies can sneeze, which will make their parents jump in surprise! Pandas drop bamboo when they die.

Foxes

Type: Passive

Foxes are tough to catch, and they're also shy. You can get them to settle down by feeding foxes sweet berries, which are also how you get them to go into love mode. They're adorable, so it might be tempting to lead one to your home. Be careful, though – they'll go after chickens, rabbits, and other small animals. Make sure your hutches are secure before bringing them to your farm. They can hold items in their mouths, and they'll drop whatever that item may be when killed.

Polar Bears

Type: Neutral/Hostile

Polar bears aren't particularly interested in you, unless you get between a parent and its cub. At that point, get ready to defend yourself. Otherwise, there's not much going on with polar bears. They can't be bred or ridden. You can use a lead on them to move them around, but what's the point? They drop cod or salmon when killed.

Dolphins

Type: Neutral

Get near a dolphin, and you'll get a temporary speed buff. Feed them cod or salmon, and they'll lead you toward the nearest shipwreck or ocean ruins. Not bad! Other than that, they're fun to watch as they jump out of the water and play with the other members of their pods. They drop raw cod when they're killed.

Turtles

Type: Passive

The most interesting thing about turtles is how closely their behavior is modeled on real-life turtles. When given seagrass, turtles will go into love mode. One will then go back to its "home beach" – no matter how far it has to travel – and then lay its eggs. Turtles have a lot of natural predators, so if you want to do a good deed, follow the mama on her journey.

Rabbits

Type: Passive

Rabbits appear in a variety of biomes. They have to be approached slowly, and can be tamed and bred by feeding them carrots, dandelions, or golden carrots. They can drop rabbit hide and raw rabbit when killed, and can rarely drop rabbit's feet.

Squid

Type: Passive

There's not much to say about these guys. They appear in oceans, beaches, and rivers, and will drop ink sacs when killed.

Food

All right! Now that we've examined Minecraft's farming and animal ecosystems a bit, it's time to look at food. Those two systems arguably intersect in one of the most important places around: your stomach. If you're playing on survival mode, you don't only have to keep track of your health. Like a lot of other games in the survival genre, your hunger gauge will slowly deplete over time. Once it's gone, your health will start to drip out as well.

If you're hungry, you eat, right? How much simpler could it be? Hold on a second. While the hunger meter and its effects are readily apparent, there's another hidden value that underpins the system. This underlying mechanic is called saturation. It might be invisible, but it's no less important than that little row of meat icons that appears on your screen. That invisible number decreases as you perform various activities around the world. Breaking bricks, sprinting, jumping, attacking enemies, and taking damage all reduce your saturation levels. When it's gone, your hunger bar will shake a little bit. At that point, you'll start to get hungry and lose icons.

It might be tempting to stuff your face with whatever's closest, but it's a bad idea in Minecraft, just as it is in the real world. Not all foods are created equal. Some are the equivalent of junk food, giving you a superficial indicator that you're full, but not contributing to the saturation values. It's basically the equivalent of scarfing down a bag of chips and then feeling hungry again in an hour. If you want to keep your belly full and your avatar in tip-top shape, there are some foods that you should definitely put on your menu, with the amount of health and saturation restorations listed in parenthesis.

The Best

Eat these when you need a boost. They offer the best balance of hunger and saturation fulfillment.

- Golden Carrot (6, 14.)
- Golden Apple (9.6, 13.6) – Adds Regeneration II effect for five seconds and Absorption for two minutes
- Enchanted Golden Apple (4, 9.6) – Adds Regeneration II for 20 seconds on Java (Regeneration IV for 30 seconds on Bedrock), Absorption IV for two minutes, Resistance for five minutes, and Fire Resistance for five minutes
- Cooked Mutton (6, 9.6)
- Cooked Porkchop (8, 12.8)
- Cooked Salmon (6, 9.6)
- Rabbit Stew (10, 12)
- Steak (8, 12.8)

Normal Foods

Make these items staples of your Minecraft diet, and you'll be living well.

- Baked Potato (5, 6)
- Beetroot Soup (6, 7.2)
- Bread (5, 6)
- Carrot (3, 3.6)
- Cooked Chicken (6, 7.2)
- Cooked Cod (5, 6)
- Cooked Rabbit (5, 6)
- Mushroom Stew (6, 7.2)
- Pumpkin Pie (8, 4.8)
- Suspicious Stew (6, 7.2) – The effects of this recipe can vary, depending on what flower you use. Good picks include Allium (Fire Resistance), Blue Orchid or Dandelion (Saturation), Cornflower (Jump Boost), Oxeye Daisy (Regeneration), and Poppy (Night Vision). Other flowers have negative effects, like Azure Bluet (Blindness), Lily of the Valley (Poison), Tulips (Weakness), and Wither Rose (Wither).

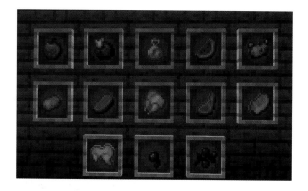

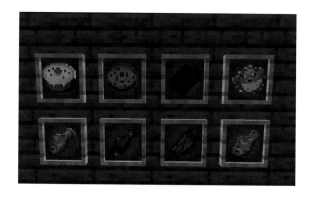

Low-Value Foods

Eat these when you're desperate, but know that better options are out there.

- Apple (4, 2.4)
- Chorus Fruit (4, 2.4) – Check your surroundings before biting into one of these. There's a chance that you might be teleported to a random spot.
- Honey Bottle (6, 2.4) – Removes poison status effects
- Melon Slice (2, 1.2)
- Poisonous Potato (2, 1.2) – Eat these, and there's a 60-percent chance you'll be poisoned for four seconds
- Potato (1, 0.6)
- Raw Beef (3, 1.8)
- Raw Chicken (2, 1.2) – There's a reason we cook poultry; eating raw chicken has a 30-percent chance of giving you the Hunger status effect for 30 seconds.
- Raw Mutton (2, 1.2)
- Raw Porkchop (1.8, 4.8)
- Raw Rabbit (3, 1.8)
- Spider Eye (2, 3.2) – Gives Poison status effect for four seconds
- Sweet Berries (2, 0.4)

These Are Technically Food

Given a choice between starving and eating this stuff, the choice is clear. Barely.

- Cake (2, 0.4 per slice; 14, 2.8 whole)
- Cookie (2, 0.4)
- Dried Kelp (1, 0.6)
- Pufferfish (1, 0.2) – Adds Hunger III status effect for 15 seconds, Nausea II for 55 seconds, and Poison IV for 60 seconds.
- Raw Cod (2, 0.4)
- Raw Salmon (2, 0.4)
- Rotten Flesh (4, 0.8) – Eating this gives an 80-percent chance of getting the Hunger status effect for 30 seconds.
- Tropical Fish (1, 0.2)

Honey Blocks Are Sweet, Too!

Honey isn't just a sweet treat in Minecraft. The Buzzy Bees update introduced bees and their sweet nectar, and it also added a new type of block with fairly wide-reaching building implications. Honey blocks have some interesting properties that set it apart from a lot of other building materials.

Since honey is sticky, it naturally makes sense for that aspect of the material to have some gameplay attached to it. Honey blocks, which can be crafted with four honey bottles, slow down anyone who walks across their sticky surface and also limit jump heights. Mobs seem to be aware of those movement-restricting properties, since they'll try to avoid walking across honey blocks whenever possible. Take advantage of that in your builds by setting up enemy-repelling barriers.

Players can climb up and down the surface of honey blocks, too, making them a potential substitute for ladders in multi-story builds or when exploring deep cave networks. You can also use them to stick along the wall in a slow-motion wall-run kind of maneuver, which is pretty fun. They'll break your fall, too, reducing the amount of damage you take if you manage to land on one.

Finally, they're similar to slime blocks in that they can be stuck to pistons and used to pull other blocks. They won't stick to slime blocks, though, which opens up some intereresting possibilities. Additionally, items that fall on honey blocks will stick to them when the blocks are moved, instead of staying in place.

Hostile Mobs and Combat

Sometimes all you want is to live a chill life. You know, walk around the garden, go horseback riding, and maybe build some nice bookshelves. Satisfying those calming impulses is why Mojang created peaceful mode. Things are a bit more rough-and-tumble throughout the rest of the game, and you're inevitably going to need to fight for your survival.

Combat has long been an essential element of Minecraft, and it's gone through some evolutions. Time was, you were able to swing your sword as quickly as you could press a button, turning your blade into a blur of destruction. In 2016, Mojang released Java version 1.9, better known as the Combat Update. This proved to be a controversial one. Players could still swing their weapons quickly, but doing so vastly reduced their effectiveness. Instead, fighting became a game of timing. Adding a cooldown was meant to add more strategy and make combat more interesting, but it ended up polarizing the community. Some liked this new facet of battling, while others decried its unintuitive nature. Meanwhile, Bedrock Edition players continued fighting the old way, without having to worry about those changes.

Mojang has continued to experiment with combat, releasing several public tests that highlight proposed changes. Some of them include adding weapon variants with different effective ranges, or simply slowing down how quickly players can swing their weapons. This isn't likely something that's going to be fully addressed anytime soon – and whatever form combat eventually takes, it's probably not going to please everyone. In the meantime, here's what you need to know about Minecraft's current arsenal, and what you can do to make it as effective as possible.

This isn't the most optimal way to fight Endermen.

Tools Of The Trade

Swords

Swords are one of Minecraft's go-to weapons, and for good reason: They're swords. They're one of the first weapons you'll probably craft in the game, and they remain a viable way to attack enemies within melee range throughout the entire experience. On Java Edition, swords have a special sweeping attack that can damage multiple enemies that are within range. All you have to do is attack with a full charge meter. Those extra enemies take less damage than the main target, but they'll get knocked back a little – perfect for controlling a crowd of mobs. Bedrock players don't get sweep attacks, but they can enjoy the knockback effects when battling enemies one-on-one. All melee weapons, including swords, can be used to perform critical hits on enemies. It's a simple maneuver: Either fall down from a height (careful!) or jump at an enemy, attacking as you descend. Nail it, and you'll net some extra damage, visually represented with a few star-like particles.

Shields

The differences between Bedrock and Java Editions are once again highlighted with how they handle shields. In both versions, the defensive items are placed in the offhand position. Java players can then manually activate them to block most incoming attacks. Arrows? Fireballs? Tridents? Melee attacks from those awful zombies? No problem. You move at a sneaking pace when your shield is outstretched, but you are safe from most incoming attacks. Java players can also decorate

them to fully express their senses of style. Bedrock functionality is a bit different. Since that version of the game is designed to be the same across platforms – including tablets with touchscreens – they're not quite as active. Instead, they're automatically equipped when you crouch. From there, they function the same way.

Axes

These melee weapons are for more than just chopping wood, even though you might only associate them with trees and lumberjacks. In Java, axes actually outperform swords in pure damage, though it comes with a slight hit to their overall speed. They also take more of a durability hit than swords when you bring them into the

battlefield. Finally, they can disable shields – perfect for PvP encounters. That's not the case in Bedrock; they're as fast as swords, but do less damage. Oh well.

Bows are a great way to take out Creepers, but don't get cocky – they can and will do their best to close the space between you.

Bows

Taking enemies out at range is satisfying, oddly because bows can be so tricky to use. The longer you hold down the attack button, the farther back you pull the string. While it's possible to shoot quickly, you'll notice that arrows fall limply to the ground and don't do as much damage as they're capable of outputting when you treat your bow like the world's worst machine gun. Even charged shots have an effective target distance, which means you'll have to aim higher to accommodate height drops when attempting longer-ranged shots. Bows need arrows, too, which can be crafted with sticks, flint, and feathers. That is, unless it's been enhanced with the Infinite enchantment.

Crossbows

Crossbows were added in the Village and Pillage update, and they can be acquired by trading with villagers or finding them in chests. They're a more deadly version of the bow, but that damage

comes with a trade-off: They take a long time to reload. If you're lucky, you can mitigate this by having several crossbows in your inventory bar. Cycle through them, firing and moving on to the next one, to create a poor-man's Gatling gun. Of course, you'll have to eventually reload, but hopefully your target won't be around to watch that part of the show.

Tridents

Drowned enemies aren't anything special, right? Waterlogged zombies? Who cares? It's easy to dismiss these guys until you find one that's wielding a trident. These weapons do a massive amount of damage, which is why you don't want to immediately dismiss Drowned on sight. Kill them, and you have a chance to claim one of these huge forks for yourself. They're interesting, because they can be thrown like spears or used as a poking melee weapon. If you throw it, you'll need to manually retrieve it – unless it's enchanted with Loyalty.

Zombies aren't particularly difficult, but don't take them lightly, either. They can call in reinforcements!

Combat Essentials

While your specific tactics may vary depending on the foe you're fighting, most of the basics still apply. If you want to win, deal damage to the bad guy while trying to avoid getting killed. Easy enough? Sarcasm aside, once you get acquainted with the fundamentals, combat really isn't that complicated. There are some differences between Java and Bedrock Editions, but much of this knowledge jumps the gap between platforms.

First things first, we were only kind of kidding when we said to try to avoid getting killed. An easy way to do that is to get out of the way of attacks before they connect. It's pretty obvious stuff, but if you haven't played before (or are a little rusty), it's probably worth taking some time to get used to

strafing away from ranged attacks, blocking with your shield, and getting in close and retreating. These moves will serve you well in the long term.

A good way to build up those fundamentals is by taking on one of Minecraft's most notorious mobs, the Creeper. Just about every novice player has had the experience of fighting a skeleton (or pig), and trying the same up-close-and-personal maneuvers with a Creeper. We all know how that ends: with an explosion. Taking these guys out at range with a bow is an easy and effective way, but it's not a bad idea to push your skills a bit. Get used to getting in close, swiping with a melee attack, and retreating from it before the "hiss" transforms into a "boom." Once you get used to doing that with Creepers, you can do the same kind of "stick and move" attacks with just about every other menace that walks the earth.

Of course, just because you can do something doesn't mean you need to. Fortnite gained attention in large part because of its build-based battles (the fact that it's free didn't hurt, either), but Minecraft did it first. Success in battle may depend on inflicting the most pain, but don't sell damage-mitigation short. One of the most

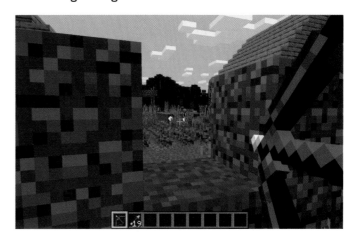

Endermen and other tall enemies can't seem to comprehend their height. Take advantage of their stupidity.

effective ways to prevent getting hurt in combat is to keep your foes at arm's length. Aside from Vexes, most enemies can't walk through solid walls. Take advantage of that by building walls to block the bad guys in. Once immobilized, you can take them out at your own leisure.

For example, Endermen and Wither Skeletons are tall, at about three blocks in height. If you place a barrier at their head level or tunnel into a wall with a two-block-high hold, they won't be able to follow you in. From there, you're free to slash them to ribbons without breaking a sweat – or losing any of your precious health. Similarly, you can build short walls that keep bad guys out, while allowing you to ascend and attack. You

know all that cobblestone you probably have in your inventory? Put it to good use!

Zombies are Minecraft's punching bags, but their ability to call in reinforcements can be a bit of a pain. If you ever feel like you're about to get swarmed or overwhelmed, you can sweep the bad guys away by dropping a bucket of water at the ground. The current will repel the enemies, giving you a chance to regroup or retreat. You are keeping a bucket of water with you, right? If you're feeling spicy, there's also the nuclear-option version of this: lava buckets. Just be warned that this should be used as an absolute last resort, since it's easy to put yourself in a bad spot and it will likely ruin any loot that the mobs drop. This is still a slightly more sensible solution when you're

above enemies and either can't line up a decent shot or you just want to watch the world burn for a minute. When you're satisfied that the lava has done its job, block it up to remove the hot threat.

There are a couple of more delicious ways to even the playing field, too. Sweet berry bushes produce a tasty treat, but their thorny branches slow down and damage most mobs – hostile and friendly. Setting up a two-deep perimeter of these plants is a solid way to set up a defense. Honey blocks also slow down mobs and prevent them from jumping. That applies to you, too, so make sure that you place these at a distance from where you plan to do your fighting, unless you want to be part of an accidentally comical performance.

Quick Hits

Much of success in Minecraft's combat comes down to getting the hang of the controls and also learning a bit more about the enemies that you're facing. Some of the hostile mobs have special qualities or properties that are worth calling out, though the bulk of the lesson with each of these remains, "Hit them a bunch, try not to get hit."

Endermen: They look scary, but they'll ignore you unless you put them in your crosshairs. From there, they'll either rush you or attempt to teleport behind you. Like we said earlier, take advantage of their height and get to where they can't reach you.

Cave Spiders: These guys spawn in abandoned mines, and are more dangerous than their vanilla Spider cousins. The reason? Their attacks are poisonous. You can either wait out the effect or remove it entirely by drinking a bucket of milk or a bottle of honey.

Ghasts: What's that giant thing in the Nether's sky? Unless we're talking about an Ender Dragon, it's probably a Ghast. They float around, occasionally throwing out explosive fireballs that pack a punch. You can block them with your shield, or, better yet, send them back from where they came with a well-timed swipe of your sword or other weapon. If it connects, it's a one-shot kill.

Evokers: These spell-casting creeps are the only way to get the Totem of Undying. Fortunately, they don't carry these life-saving items in their off-hands. They cast spells and summon Vexes, tiny little flying pests that can follow you through walls. Evokers are a pain on their own, but Vexes can quickly overwhelm you if you aren't careful. Take them out at range, if you can.

Witches: If you've seen their swampy huts, you may be close to their occupant. Witches may look like villagers, but they're far less friendly. They'll throw debuffing potions at you while buffing themselves with healing potions and other beneficial brews. Wear them down with arrows, unless you're well-armored and impatient. They're worth fighting, since they often drop a nice variety of rare alchemical ingredients.

Withers: You have to want to fight these guys, since they only appear after summoning them. If you want to fight one of the toughest mobs in the game, arrange four blocks of soul sand in a T shape, and place three Wither Skeleton skulls (found from the mobs in Nether fortresses) on the top three blocks. This monster creates a ton of damage after it appears, so retreat the second you spawn it. Then do your best to pick it off from a distance. When it's down to about half of its health, it'll enter a phase where only melee attacks will do damage. It's best to take this mob on in a tunnel deep underground, where its flying ability is hindered. Bedrock Edition players face an even harder battle. In the second phase of battle, it will explode, summon several wither skeletons, and rush at you. Good luck.

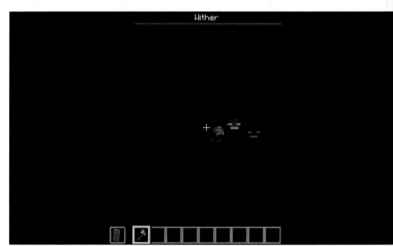

Ender Dragon: This guy is basically Minecraft's boss, and he's the first not-so-friendly face you'll spot when entering The End. He's surrounded by loads of Endermen, and a ring of obsidian towers. On top of these towers are End Crystals, which will heal the dragon when he flies by. Destroy these by shooting them with arrows when you can. A few are in iron cages, which will require you to carefully build up to them and break through. Careful though: end crystals explode with the power of a Creeper, so get some space between you and it. Once all the crystals are destroyed, you can focus on the Ender Dragon. Fire arrows when you can, and avoid its attacks – unlike the Ghast's fireballs, you can't bat these back to its sender. The dragon will land from time to time, giving you a chance to slash at it with your melee weapon. Be patient and well outfitted, and you'll probably end up surviving. Good luck!

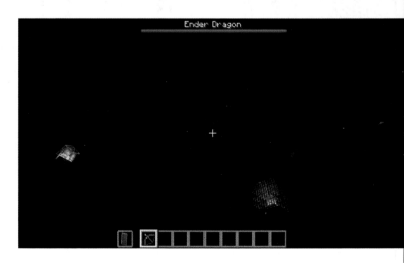

Points of Interest

Minecraft's worlds are procedurally generated, meaning that every rock, tree, and mob that you encounter has been plopped into existence by following a complicated series of rules. That part of what makes exploring so exciting; you really never know exactly what you're going to find out there. As interesting as floating mountains and gigantic lava waterfalls can be, players can find some other locations that are worth checking out. These places are an abundant source of special blocks, treasure, and potentially deadly situations. See something that looks a bit more structured on the horizon or under the water's surface? Here's what you need to know before venturing further.

Shipwrecks

Located In: Beaches, islands, or in the ocean

Your little rowboat may be significantly smaller than these vessels, but you have one key advantage: You're still floating. Whoever once sailed these ships is long gone, which gives you a chance to play out your pirate fantasies. Well, so long as your pirate fantasies only revolve around plunder; you can't pilot these ships, unfortunately. Despite their nonfunctional nature, they're still worth a quick bit of exploration.

Shipwrecks usually contain several chests in the hold and some of the other below-deck rooms. If you're lucky, one of them might contain a map to a hidden treasure. Follow it, and you're on your way to riches and glory. If you're on Java Edition, you can change your language options to Pirate, if you want to fully embrace the fantasy. Aaar!

TIP Old-school Minecrafters might think they can be sneaky and use doors, torches, and other blocks to create pockets of breathable air underwater. Unfortunately, these techniques no longer work. If you want to fully explore undersea attractions in updated versions of the game, you're either going to need to move quickly or track down some water-breathing potions.

Witch Huts

Located In: Swamps

Swamps are a great place to call home in Minecraft, so it shouldn't be surprising to learn that someone has beaten you to it. Witch Huts can be found in these biomes. They're home to – you guessed it – Witches. They're not particularly social, so they may not be around if you go inside. If they are, however, they're not going to be happy at your unannounced visit.

Whether or not a Witch is home, the interiors should be the same. Key items of note include a cauldron and crafting table and a black cat. On Bedrock Edition, the cauldron will contain a random potion. Java players will have to make do with the fact that they're inside a Witch's Hut.

TIP Witches may look harmless, but they're quite eager to toss potions at you to even out the playing field. Take these creepy mobs out at range, or do your best to avoid getting hit – and debuffed – by their wicked brews.

Igloos

Located In: Snowy tundra and snowy taiga

These snowy structures don't have a lot to offer on the surface. You'll find a bed and furnace inside, perfect for warming up and dozing off. Once you're recharged, you can use the crafting table. Time to move along, right? Not so fast!

About half of the time, these little buildings have a secret. Look under one of the carpet blocks or dig carefully down (Not straight down! Never straight down!), and you might find a shaft that leads to a basement. Here, it gets a little weird. You'll come across a pair of mobs in cages, one villager and one zombie villager. There should be an apple and a potion of weakness inside the igloo, which you can use to cure the infected mob. Once they're both released, the villagers will get to work at the brewing stand and cauldron. Ta-dah! Now you have access to a cleric and a leatherworker.

Jungle Temples

Located In: Jungles

If movies have taught us anything, it's that jungle temples are completely safe places to explore, and that they're never filled with traps. OK, maybe we've been watching the wrong movies. These structures look like ancient stone pyramids, and they're definitely worth a visit – so long as you watch your step.

If you look along the floor as you creep along, you'll notice some tripwires stretched across the floor. Smash or avoid them, unless you'd like to be pelted with arrows. Deeper inside, there's a switch-based puzzle. Pull the levers in the correct order, and the treasure is yours! Or you can just smash your way through the wall and take it that way. Regardless of what method you choose, treasure is always welcome. Just don't dwell on all the bones, lest you start feeling guilty...

Beware of this drop!

Desert Temples

Located In: Deserts

As with the igloo, there doesn't seem to be much going on in these structures at first glance. Head inside the main interior chamber, and you'll see several colored blocks arranged in a pattern. They're not just decorative – they're a clue!

Directly below that pattern is a long drop that leads to four treasure chests. Not bad, right? Not so fast! If you're not careful, you'll activate the pressure plate at the bottom of this vertical tunnel, detonating several hidden blocks of TNT. In the extremely unlikely event that you survive, that treasure is gone. Oops. Instead, you can slowly descend with a series of well-placed blocks, or you can drop water from the top (Always bring a water bucket!) and head down in style. Break the pressure plate, and plunder away.

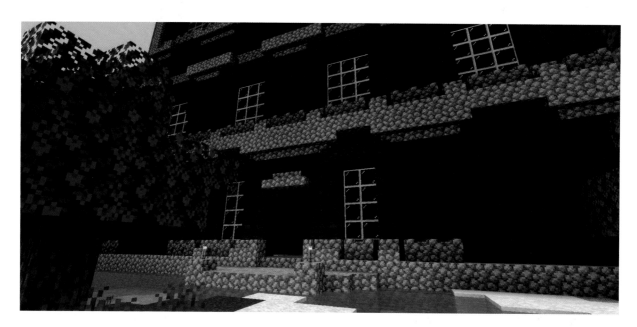

Woodland Mansions

Located In: Dark oak forests

You might stumble across one of these places while exploring forests, but there's another way: Cartographer villagers can offer woodland-explorer maps as trades, which will direct you toward the nearest one. These are tough, so however you get there, make sure that you're well-stocked and ready for the worst. Woodland Mansions are large and filled with some of the most annoying mobs in the games, but they're also a great place to loot. Of course they are.

These mansions are essentially dungeons built from a palette of different room options. In other words, each one is going to be different, but if you raid enough of them you might start recognizing some familiar-looking spots. The first thing you'll

notice after walking through the front door is that these places are dark – even if the sun is out. Place torches as you venture forth, to prevent additional mobs from spawning as you proceed. You're going to have your hands full, as it is, without having to worry about a run-of-the mill Creeper or Spider popping up from a corner behind you.

Woodland Mansions are home to two particularly annoying mobs, Illagers and Evokers. Since they're related to villagers, you should hear their annoyed murmuring before you see them. If you can, take them out at a distance. Illagers can easily be blocked in if you can make a quick pillar and get above their melee range. From there, box them in and you're set. If you have a name tag that you're willing to use, if you name an Illager "Johnny" a la *The Shining*, then the axe-wielding maniacs will target all nearby mobs, and not just you. Evokers are, well, Evokers. Use your bow to get them before they spot you and you're golden. Otherwise, their Vex minions can easily overwhelm you.

There'd better be something worthwhile to make up for all this trouble, right? Heck yeah! Woodland Mansions contain loads of treasure chests, some of which may contain enchanted items. Plus, when it's cleared, you have a pretty swanky multilevel home to call your own.

Ocean Monuments

Located In: Oceans

Ocean Monuments are among the trickiest places to tackle in Minecraft, thanks to the fact that they're underwater. If you don't have depth-strider boots, an aqua-affinity helmet, and plenty of water-breathing potions, these are going to be an exceptional challenge. Proceed at your own risk.

If you can't find one of these places on your own (They're fairly easy to spot, even from beaches), you can trade cartographer villagers for an ocean-explorer map that should set you straight. Look around for a large archway, which should lead to the monument's interior. The goal here is to work your way through the maze-like interior to find and defeat the three Elder Guardians.

Being underwater for an extended period of time is tricky enough, but the Elder Guardians have an ability that makes it even trickier: They can hit you with a mining-fatigue status effect, which prevents you from breaking blocks for five minutes. So much for bashing your way through the place. When elder guardians have their spikes out, hold your fire – any attacks you do during that time will come back to you via thorn damage. The place is also infested with regular Guardians, who blast you with laser-like beams. Break line of sight before it charges, or prepare to take a fairly significant hit.

Once the final Elder Guardian is down and the status effect is gone for good, get ready to mine. Ocean monuments are the only place you can get prismarine blocks and, if you have a silk-touch pickax, sea lanterns. Also, there's an obelisk-like structure in one of the main halls. Break through the dark prismarine blocks, and you'll be rewarded with eight gold blocks. Awesome! Just don't think too hard about how you can swim with all that gold in your pocket.

Break inside this structure for a lucrative surprise.

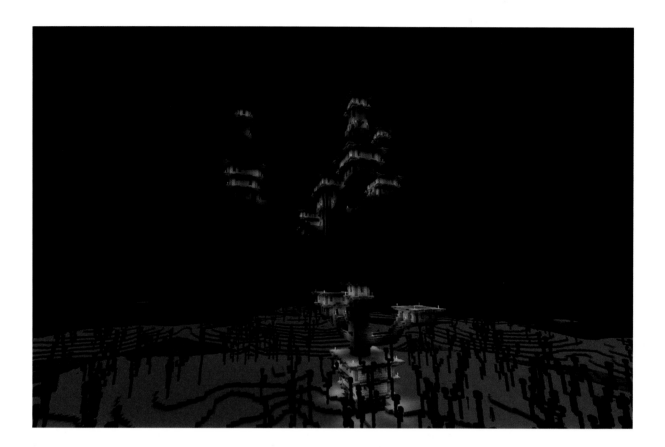

End Cities and End Ships

Located In: The End

After you beat the Ender Dragon, you'll probably want to leave The End and get back to greener pastures. Not so fast! If you haven't explored this place further, you're missing out on one of the game's best treasures. For real. To get there, throw an ender pearl into the portal that appears after you defeat the Ender Dragon.

The End doesn't look like much, and finding an End City is probably going to require some perseverance. Pick a direction and start walking. Build some pillars with torches every once in a while, to keep you from losing your way, since you can easily get lost here if you aren't careful. Eventually, you'll (hopefully) encounter an End City.

These places look like one of Dr. Seuss' nightmares, with weird towers and strange, bulbous outcrops. The biggest danger are the wall-mounted Shulkers. Thanks to the strange geometry, their levitation-inducing projectiles can create some real problems for you if you aren't being careful. Approach carefully, and try to get in a doorway before engaging them.

Occasionally, you'll see a giant ship docked near an End City. This is the big one. Carefully work your way inside, and you'll find treasure as well as the big prize: Elytra, a chest-mounted pair of wings that let you glide down. If you use fireworks while you're gliding, you'll get a boost upward, essentially allowing you to fly. It's one of the fastest ways to get around, so make a beeline for these as soon as you can.

Break this frame to claim your Elytra.

Villagers (and Pillagers)

Mojang upped its social game in 2018 with the release of Minecraft version 1.14, perhaps better known as the Village & Pillage update. Most notably, it gave players a reason to hang around in villages, thanks to an updated trading system. Fans may have enjoyed the quality-of-life improvements, but it did bring its share of drama. Fortunately, it was confined within the boundaries of the game. As much as Minecrafters might enjoy spending time with the villagers, there are some other folks who can't stand 'em. In this section, we'll explore the new systems, including how to deal with these pesky Illagers.

Chapter 7: Villagers (and Pillagers)

Villages often have farms, which can be a great way to get a head start in your early game.

Before we turn our attention toward their nasty counterparts, let's run down the basics (and not-so-basics) of villages and villagers. Villages can spawn in plains, desert, savanna, taiga, and snowy tundra biomes, with each type bringing along its own cosmetic flair. Though they may be built from different materials, they're functionally identical communities that serve – for the most part – as peaceful little refuges against the often harsh outside.

Villages are home to NPCs known as villagers. These mobs will leave you alone as they go about their business, wandering around, gossiping with their friends, going to work, and sleeping. You might not be able to decipher their weird little murmurings, but they speak the universal language of commerce. That's one of the main reasons these little communities can be worth seeking out.

There are several types of villagers, and each location randomly spawns in a selection of the characters. Though they have jobs and can be used for trading, don't even think about attacking them. Well, you're welcome to think about it, but be aware of the consequences: They don't drop items or XP, and all you can accomplish is aggravating them to a point where they'll sic their iron golems on you. Ultimately, if you want to be mischievous, sheathe your sword and loot their homes and other structures. You'll potentially find some great items, they don't get upset, and you still can feel as though you've gotten in your daily amount of mischief.

Villagers are friendly, so don't bother attacking them. You won't gain anything other than the ire of their friends.

When you're ready to go legit, interact with them. That will bring up a trading interface. Each villager type has a pool of potential trades that they draw from, ranging from fairly awful to quite good. You'll never know until you try, so be sure to chat with every villager you come across, at least once.

Even if a villager has mediocre trades, there's something you can do about it: When you make trades with a villager, they'll slowly level up in rank, which unlocks better and better potential trades. They start off as novices but can be promoted to apprentice, journeyman, expert, and master levels, provided you pony up. Trades are simple. Each villager has a small list of things they want, and what they'll trade for it. For instance, librarians will often trade paper for other coveted items. If you have a home-base setup that lets you mass manufacture paper, that's a pretty sweet deal. Other deals, such as a fisherman who cooks salmon for you in exchange for emeralds – one of the villagers' highly prized currencies – isn't worth the trouble.

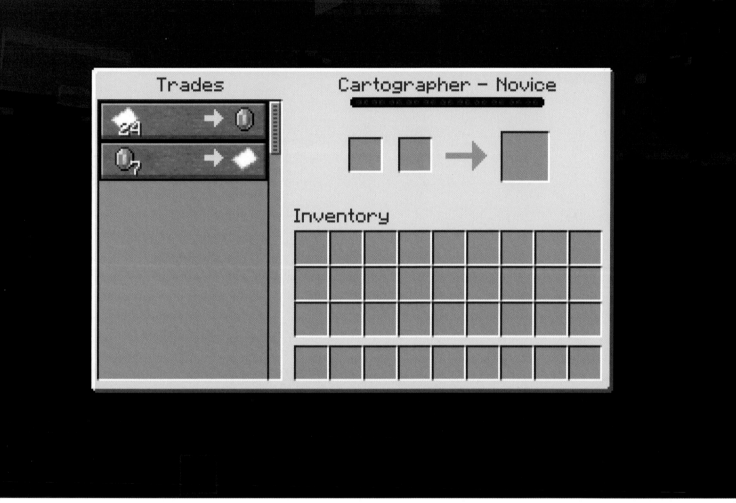

More trades will unlock as you level up your trade relationships. Don't be dismayed if the first few options aren't great.

When you make a lot of trades with an individual villager, there's a chance that the trade will temporarily lock up. Leave them alone for a bit, and they'll refill their inventories (something that's visually represented by little swirls that appear over the character). They'll refill twice a day, and then you'll need to give them a break before they're ready for that particular trade again. Trade rates can fluctuate, too, so if something is interesting but out of your price range, check back. There's a chance that they might cut prices if nobody is interested in their wares.

There are too many potential trades to fully get into here, but each type of villager has a fairly easy to understand inventory type. Once you get the hang of what each job is about, you'll have a solid sense of what to expect when you interact with them. Here's a quick rundown of the jobs, their associated workstations, and a general trade-type overview.

1 Armorer (Blast Furnace)

Looking for armor? This is a pretty safe bet. Low-level trades are fairly mundane, but leveled-up armorers can offer enchanted diamond gear. They're also one of the only ways to get bells, which can be rung to motivate villagers to get inside their homes. Blast furnaces are specialized furnaces that let you refine ore at a faster rate than ordinary ones.

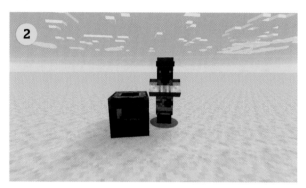

2 Butcher (Smoker)

Butchers are a decent source of meat, which makes them pretty useless. Unless you're in dire straits, there are much easier and cheaper ways to get your hands on what they have to offer. Smokers can be used to rapidly cook meat.

3 Cartographer (Cartography Table)

These guys are a great place to visit if you're ready to do some exploring. They can sell treasure maps to ocean monuments and woodland mansions. They're also the exclusive sellers of the globe banner pattern, for those banner completionists out there. Cartography tables allow you to copy, expand, and lock maps.

4 Cleric (Brewing Stand)

Have you been killing a lot of zombies? Are you swimming in zombie flesh? First, gross. With that out of the way, clerics will exchange your unused zombie flesh for potions, glowstones, and a high-end drink that gives XP. You're probably not using zombie flesh for anything else, so you may as well get something for it. Brewing stands are used to make potions.

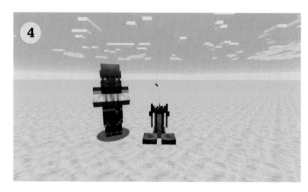

5 Farmer (Composter)

Minecraft farmers have a lot of food, unsurprisingly, which makes them a great trader. They're also not particularly observant, so you can raid their nearby farms and sell them back their own vegetables for emeralds. You can put unwanted food items in the composter to turn them into bone meal.

6 Fisherman (Barrel)

Fisherman sell fish, which should come as no surprise. They also can cell enchanted rods, and will inexplicably buy boats for emeralds. Barrels are just a storage item. Sorry.

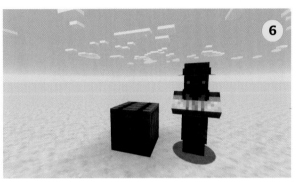

7 Fletcher (Fletching Table)

You want bows, crossbows, both normal and enchanted? This is the villager for you. They'll also sell tipped arrows, which are arrows that have been imbued with potion effects. Fletching tables currently have no player functionality. Sorry again.

8 Leatherworker (Cauldron)

Leather armor is a dime a dozen, but don't let the leatherworker's early trades turn you off. Eventually, they'll start trading saddles and enchanted leather gear. It might not be the best, but it could be worse (looking at you, fisherman). Cauldrons can be used to remove dye from items on Java Edition. On Bedrock, they can be used to hold dyed water or lava, upgrade potions, and tip arrows with potion effects.

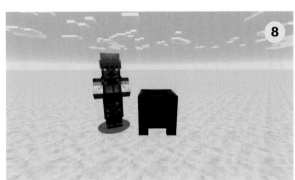

9 Librarian (Lectern)

Consider yourself lucky if you find a librarian with good trades. Even the mediocre ones are worth keeping around, thanks to the potential of their late-game trades of enchanting books. These books are the only way you can get the mending enchant, one of the best possible item enchants around. You can put books on lecterns, which allows other players to read them.

10 Mason (Stonecutter)

Masons are worth engaging with if you're desperately low on building materials (or are seeking ones from undiscovered or out-of-the way biomes), but they don't have much to offer aside from large quantities of blocks. Stonecutters let you craft smaller quantities of blocks and also removes several steps when crafting more complex stone items like chiseled stone bricks.

11 Shepherd (Loom)

The lowly shepherd has the most potential trade options, thanks to the sheer number of dyes and varieties of colored wool that Minecraft offers. They also can trade a painting. Look, we didn't say they were the best, just that he had the most options. You can use the loom to apply patterns to banners.

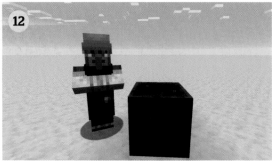

12 Toolsmith (Smithing Table)

Toolsmiths are another way to get a bell or to trade tools. At the smithing table, use a netherite ingot to upgrade diamond items to the ultimate netherite gear.

13 Weaponsmith (Grindstone)

You're not going to believe this, but the weaponsmith has a lot of different weapons to trade – normal ones, and enchanted ones. They're also happy to trade bells. The grindstone can be used to repair or disenchant tools and weapons.

Nitwits (None)

Nitwits are just along for the ride. Their profession is no profession.

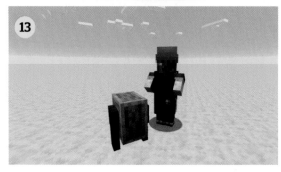

Villagers can be easily nudged into boats.

Villagers have homes, but that doesn't mean that they're not willing to move. If you find a villager that you trade with often, it might be worth relocating them closer to your home base. The easiest way is to nudge them into a boat, get into the boat, and row your way back to where you want to go – even on land. Yes, it might take a while.

Once you get them where you want them to be, it might be wise to pen them inside safely, with blocks or other object that they can't navigate over. Villagers have a tendency to wander around, which can put them in harm's way. You don't want that now, especially after rowing a boat cross-country! Villagers can also be encouraged to have little villagers by giving them access to food (drop it near them, and they'll pick it up) as well as beds for

them, their partner, and soon-to-be baby. If all goes well, hearts will appear over their heads and you'll soon have a little one. Once it grows up, they'll have a profession of their own – provided they have access to a crafting station.

You might come upon some zombie villagers out in the wild or, worse, have members of your village infected by zombies if you're playing on hard difficulty mode. While it may be tempting to put them out of their misery, they can be cured. To do so, surround the infected villager with iron bars, hit them with a splash potion of weakness, and give them a golden apple. After a few minutes, they'll be back to normal – or as normal as a villager can get.

During your explorations, you might come across hostile villager-like mobs. These are Illagers, and they come in several different varieties. The one thing they share is their dislike for players and villagers. If you stumble upon one of their watchtower-like bases, approach with caution: Defeating the mobs here is how you start a raid, which is something you may or may not want to do.

In particular, killing the patrol leader will give you the Bad Omen effect, which lasts for 100 minutes. At that point, entering a friendly village will flag it for invasion. You'll hear a horn, and then see

a meter at the top of the screen indicating the combined strength of the current raiders. Get ready to rumble!

Raiders can include run-of-the-mill Illagers, the crossbow-wielding Pillagers, witches, ravager beasts, and evokers. They'll target you and the villagers – and it's over if a villager gets taken out. These battles can be tough enough without having to worry about protecting your buddies. Fortunately, there are a few steps you can take to make survival a lot easier.

1. Protect Your Village

There are a lot of different ways to do this. Even if you don't want to start scrapping with the Illagers, it's not a bad idea to wall off the village with a partition of at least two blocks high. That, along with adding plenty of torches, should keep the mobs at bay. You can bolster those defenses by adding damage-inducing blocks like cacti, magma, or even sweet-berry bushes. Any mobs that come into contact with these will take damage; that includes villagers, too, so be extra careful.

2. Lock 'Em Up

Illagers can't kill what they can't reach, with the notable exception of the Evokers and their Vex minons. Another way to keep your villagers safe is to follow them as they go into their homes and block the doors. They can't get out and, more importantly, the bad guys can't get in. Waiting around can be tedious, so look around for the town's bell. It should be in a central location. When you ring it, villagers will run to their homes. Follow them there, and block them inside. It's for their own good, honest.

3. Gear Up

This almost goes without saying, but survival is largely dependent on your gear. If you don't have decent armor and weapons, you're probably going to get your rear end handed to you. There are ways to get around this, such as mass-producing an army of iron golems to do your dirty work for you, but all those iron blocks and jack-o-lanterns are going to be expensive. Unless you just want to watch the show, it makes more sense to take the time to

stock up on arrows and get some nicely enchanted weapons and armor – something that should realistically be a priority whether or not you want to participate in raids.

Once the last wave is defeated, the Bad Omen effect is removed and replaced with the Hero of the Village buff. The villagers are stoked that you were able to help, and will give you discounts on their trades. Just don't tell them that you're technically responsible for the attack in the first place. There's no reason to bring down the mood. On Java Edition, villagers will also show their gratitude by showering you with gifts – literally. These items might not all be great, but it's the thought that counts.

Important Builds

Did you know that you can build things in Minecraft? Crazy, right?! The thing is, with so many different components to craft and collect, just knowing that you can put them together to make something new might not be enough. Sometimes it's helpful to get some inspiration – whether you're just starting out and trying to get your bearings or haven't played for a while and aren't quite sure what to make of all these newfangled building blocks. In this chapter, we'll run through several important builds.

These are important for several reasons. First, they're a great way to easily generate some important resources, either automatically or more efficiently than you might ordinarily find. They also cover some of Minecraft's key building concepts, so once you roll through these you'll be ready to take on your own constructs. In that regard, we'll wrap up with some of the other relatively recent NPC and block interactions that you can take advantage of yourself.

Build One:
The Cow Hole

OK, this might not be the most elegant name, but it's certainly accurate. If you're looking for leather and raw steaks, you're also looking for cows. Sure, you can breed them in a pen and manually harvest them, but that can take time. There's an easier way that's also been around in Minecraft since, well, forever. Welcome to the cow hole.

To start, dig out a section of earth two blocks wide and two blocks deep. In the bottom, place a chest with a hopper feeding directly into it (check to make sure the little feeder-tube thing is connected, otherwise it won't work). Put an upside-down staircase above the chest, and then put four blocks around the hopper in a plus-sign shape. Lead at least two cows into this hole (this part requires patience), then seal them in with a single fencepost above the center (you'll have to connect it there from one of the four blocks).

Next, pull out some wheat, and feed the cows. They'll have a baby. This part requires more patience. Keep feeding and breeding the cows. Eventually, they'll reach the maximum number of mobs that can occupy a single block, and one of the older cows will die. Their leather and meat will fall into the hopper and feed into the chest. This is a good one to set up early, where you can go through the feeding process when you pass by. Waiting for a calf to grow up takes time, and you've got better things to do.

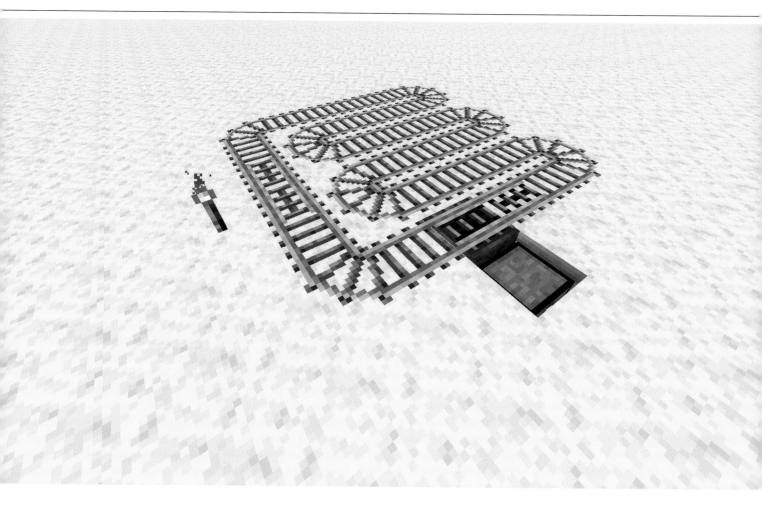

Build Two:
The Campfire Cooker

Sorry, steak tartare fans; you'll want to cook the beef before eating it. You can do it with your furnace or the more-efficient smoker, but there's a flashier way to get the perfect sear. And it's from a

place you might not expect. First, lay out a winding 6-by-6 track with a couple of powered rails, with the track running over a buried hopper feeding into a buried chest. Pop down a minecart with a hopper, and power the powered rail with redstone. Above this, place a 4-by-4 array of campfires. Toss your steaks on 'em, and get ready for a barbecue.

Each campfire can hold four steaks, and they're cooked simultaneously. We'll admit that this is pretty gimmicky, especially since some of the steaks are likely to fly onto the ground when they're done. Most will get picked up by your railcar and deposited in the chest, though. Better still, campfires don't require any fuel to work. It's fast and fun – what more could you want? Especially if you don't mind floor steaks. Does the five-second rule apply to Minecraft?

Build Three: The Time Shaver

Wool is another important resource, so you may as well work to get as much as you can. Or you could... not work to get as much as you can. This quick build will get you a reliable source of the stuff without having to do anything beyond the initial construction. Start out by placing an observer behind a grass block, with a dispenser above the observer. Behind those, place another block of your choice, with some redstone on it to power it all. Put a pair of shears inside the dispenser.

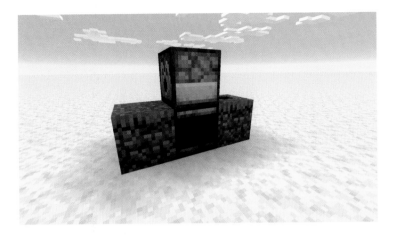

Put a hopper feeding into a chest two blocks below the grass block. Place a rail on top of the hopper (you might have to crouch first), and then put a minecart with a hopper atop that rail. Minecart hoppers have the interesting property of being able to collect items through solid blocks, which explains the odd setup. Seal it all up, making sure that you can still access the chest. Then put four glass blocks around the grass block. Lead a sheep into that tiny greenhouse, and give it a quick manual shear before capping off your construction with another glass block so your livestock can't escape.

The sheep will eat the grass, which will magically allow it to grow a new coat. The observer block notices the grass is gone, and it will dispense the shears – which will give the sheep a quick haircut. The wool falls down into the chest, and the process repeats. It's fairly slow, so you might want to consider building several if you need mass quantities of wool. You can also place a hopper into the dispenser and fill it with shears, so they'll be replaced when they break. Not too baaaaad. Sorry.

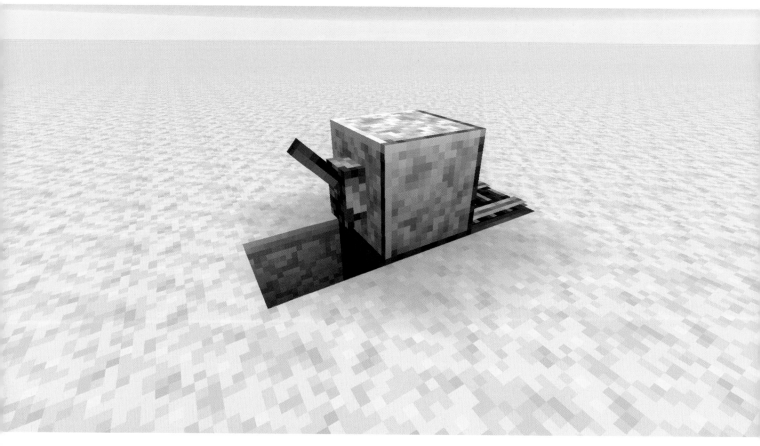

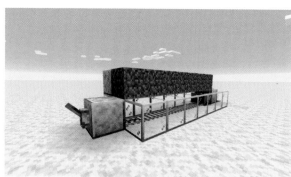

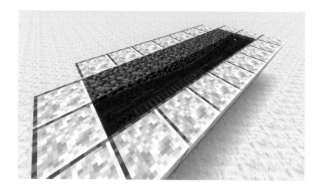

Build Four:
Automated Sugar Shack

Sugar cane is a super valuable resource, particularly if you find a villager with good paper trades. Tending a garden is satisfying in its own way, but so is building a contraption that does it all for you. Start off by burying a hopper that feeds into a barrel. Put a powered rail onto that hopper, with another block on top of the barrel. Unlike chests, you can open barrels even if something is directly above it – no lid, no problem. Put a lever on that block. Create a section of rail leading to another chunk of powered rail with a block and lever. How long you make this is up to you; it'll determine how much sugar you can grow at once.

Block off both sides of the rail with glass blocks, and put a row of blocks (whatever type you think looks good) above one side, with a row of dirt next to that. Continue blocking around the area to make a long trench. Drop water sources on both ends so the dirt gets wet. Put a row of blocks above the water, with a row of pistons on top of those.

Above the pistons put at least one observer block facing out toward the dirt, with a row of redstone connecting the rest of the blocks. The observer will keep watch, and activate the pistons if anything happens to obstruct its view. What could that be...?

Plant your sugar cane in the dirt, and be patient. Once the cane reaches the observer's height, it'll get punched by the pistons, whereupon the minecart will collect and deposit the harvest (moment of truth: flip those levers!). You can use this same basic principal with bamboo, too, to create an autosmelter setup. Just replace the crop and have the bamboo feed into furnaces instead of chests, and you'll have an unlimited source of fuel for smelting.

Build Five:
The Egg To Belly
Chicken Cooker

All right, this is a little more complicated than the others, but it'll give you an endless supply of roast chicken and feathers once it's complete. People have been automating this kind of farm for ages, but we think this is the best way to do it. First bury a chest next to a hopper, with a rail on the hopper. Put a minecart with hopper on the rail, and then carefully break the rail. Then create a pillar of sand next to the minecart and place a sand block directly above the cart. The sand will drop and clip through the minecart. Perfect! Destroy the two sand blocks, leaving the one that's now somehow part of your minecart.

Put a slab on top of the sand, with a dispenser looking into the slab. Behind the dispenser, put a comparator, with an observer one block above that comparator facing away from the dispenser. On the other side of the comparator, put an observer facing the back of the dispenser. Below it, put down a sticky piston.

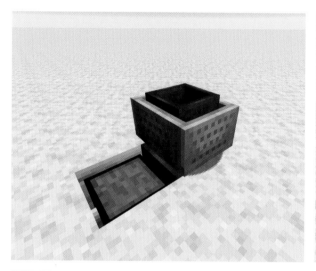

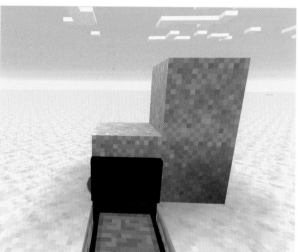

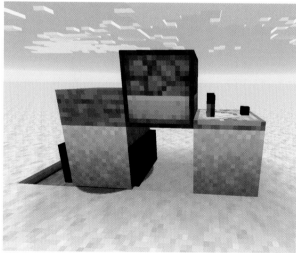

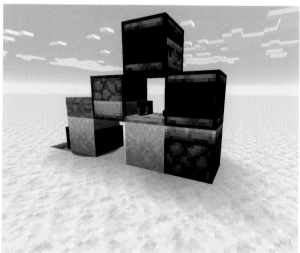

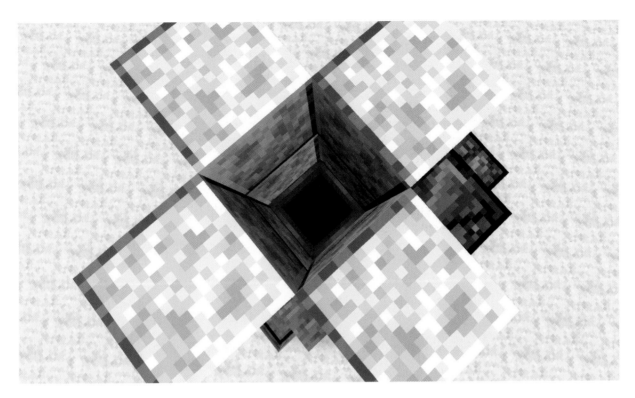

This is the hopper, where you can lure chickens into their new home or smash eggs to get them.

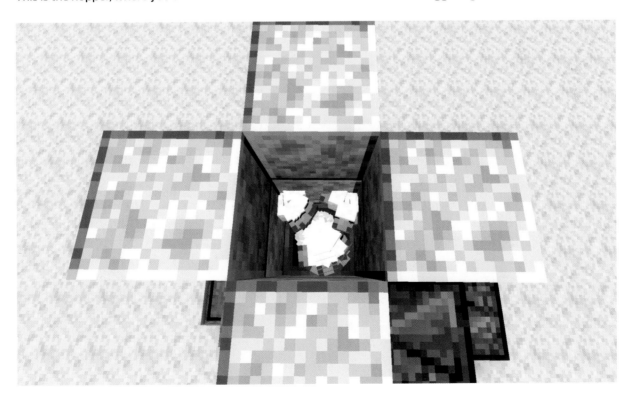

Facing the chest, put a hopper on the left side of the dispenser. Wall the hopper off with two-blocks all around (in a plus-sign shape). This is going to be where you put the chickens. You can either lead chickens into this area (building some disposable stairs) or spam a bunch of eggs into the makeshift pen until you have a bunch of cluckers. Put a block on top of the pen.

We're in the home stretch! Surround the slab with glass blocks all the way around, then drop a lava source into the glass bowl. Cap it off with a glass block, and you're set. Now all you have to do is wait. The chickens will lay eggs, which will be thrown into the dispenser. Most will break, but some will hatch into new chickens. The chicks will be fine beneath the lava, but once they reach maturity they'll bonk their heads on the surface and get cooked. Their meat and feathers will be deposited in the chest for you to collect later. Bon appetit!

Other Interesting Interactions

We're obviously just barely scratching the surface of what's possible in Minecraft – people have built working versions of Pokémon in the game, for crying out loud. Rather than walk you through these next builds step by step, here are some of the key mechanics behind them so you can figure them out for yourselves.

- **Bubble Elevator.** Waterfalls have been used to reach second stories in homes and other builds for about as long as Minecraft has been around. The Aquatic Update introduced some changes that allow users to create water elevators that function like their drier real-world counterparts. When it's underwater, soul stone blocks will create bubbles that float people upward. On the other hand, magma blocks will pull people down. Using pistons, you can create a button-operated contraption that lifts or lowers users – just make sure you're crouched on the way down, so you don't take magma damage.

- **One-Block High Hideouts.** A while back, Mojang introduced swimming animations. You can't swim on the ground, but if your character gets squished by a piston you can crawl. Take advantage of this by building a one-block-high hideout. There's no real reason to do this aside from it being strange and fun, but that's reason enough. If you're feeling particularly ambitious, you can automate the process by activating it via a pressure plate – or a motion-detector version that uses a pufferfish. Get too close, and the pufferfish inflates, triggering the piston that squishes you so you can enter.

- **Iron Farms.** These are kind of a pain to set up, but they're worth it. If four villagers are attacked or threatened by the same hostile mob within a certain span of time, they'll summon an iron golem to come to their rescue. You can take advantage of this behavior by creating four little pens with beds and workstations, with a zombie safely imprisoned nearby. Create some kind of water funnel that leads the ill-fated golem to lava doom, and you'll be swimming in iron in no time flat.

- **Switchable Nether Portal.** Nether portals are great to have around, but they're kind of noisy. You can rig up an on-off switch for them by hooking up pistons with dispensers, that either dispense flint and steel (to activate them) or water (to shut them down). That way, you can enjoy your portal without having to listen to its constant droning.

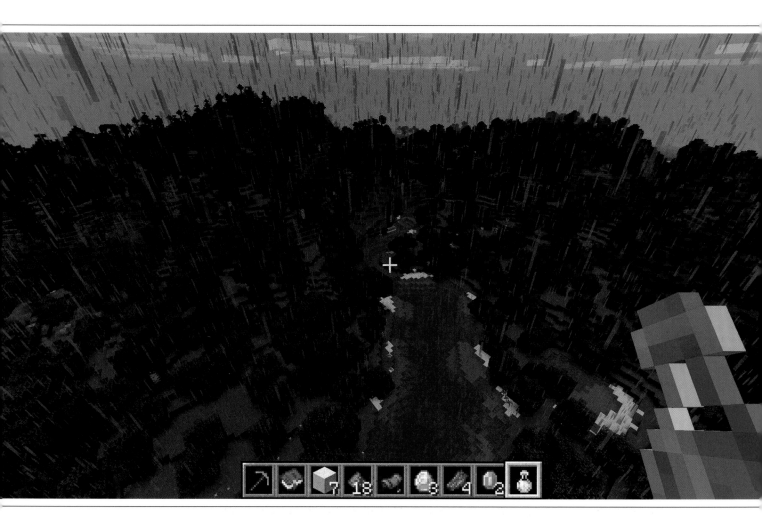

Enchanting and Potions

It's a big, dangerous world out there, and sometimes you need an edge. Having a diamond sword is a start, but eventually you'll start to feel as though you aren't living up to your Minecraft potential. Mining and farming can feel inefficient, and tougher enemies may make you want to go back to bed – and stay there. Fortunately, there's hope. Players can access a wide array of ways to equalize the playing field, by enchanting their items and brewing up special potions that provide temporary buffs. Here's what you need to know.

Building in the open air looks nice, but it's not the smartest play when Creepers are around.

Enchanting

If you're playing in Survival, you've undoubtedly noticed those green orbs that magically appear when you defeat mobs, mine ore, cook up some meat – basically, just about everything you do in the game. Those experience orbs help full up your XP meter, which appears right over your health bar, with each filled meter granting you a level.

Leveling doesn't function like it does in a lot of other RPGs. You don't become a more efficient miner or suddenly realize how to better wield your sword in combat (use the pointy end!) with progression. Instead, you can think about each level as adding another buck to your bank account. And,

as luck would have it, enchanting is what you're going to spend your hard-won wages on.

There are several ways you can unlock enchants, but the one you'll probably rely on most (at least until you're late in your Minecraft career) is through the use of an enchanting table. Look in your recipe book for the materials, and build yourself one of those, preferably inside your home base. Enchanting isn't cheap, but it's also one of the best ways to power up your character. Just to emphasize those startup costs, you won't fully realize the potential of that enchanting table until after you place 15 bookshelves around your table, one block away from the table. While you can certainly get started without that step, you'll only have access to low-level enchants.

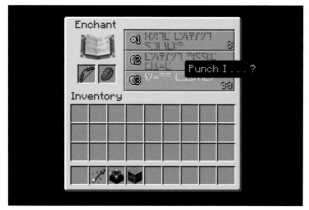

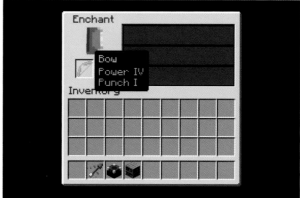

Once you're set up, enchanting is fairly self-explanatory. When you interact with the table, you'll see a list of potential enchants on the right side, with a couple of empty slots on the left. Don't panic: The text on those enchants is a cipher, and you're not meant to read what it says (though you can crack it yourself by looking up the key online). There should be three tiers of enchants listed, ranked from least powerful (and expensive) to its top-tier offering. The numbers on the right show how many levels you'll need to spend to create the enchant, with 30 being the current maximum. You'll also need some lapis lazuli. Did we already say that enchanting is expensive?

The tricky thing about enchanting is that the selection of three enchants are randomized when you first start, with new effects cycled through when you enchant an item. The offerings also rotate when you put different items on the table. For example, if you put a sword on the table, you might see that the table is offering smite, knockback, or bane of arthropods. Put boots on there, and you might be able to pick between depth strider, protection, or unbreakable. Until you commit to one of those enchantments, those will be the choices for your sword or boots. After enchanting one of those, the potential enchants will cycle anew and potentially give you different options.

Once you're ready, pop in the item you want to enchant and required lapis, pick the enchantment you're interested in, and let 'er rip. Sometimes, you might get a bonus enchantment (or more) for your trouble, too. Nice!

The anvil is another important enchanting component. This station lets you repair enchanted items by combining them, provided they're the same type of item; you can't repair a sword's durability with a bow. It's also where you can use enchanted books, which are items that give you a clear description of what enchant you'll get by combining it with an item at an anvil. Books are currently the only way you can get the coveted "mending" enchant, so be on the lookout!

With more than two dozen possible enchants, the obvious question is: "Which ones are best?" Let's go through them all. Along with their names and descriptions, we're putting down their maximum level, since some enchants have different potential rankings, the higher, the better. There aren't any "bad" enchants, but some are more situational than others.

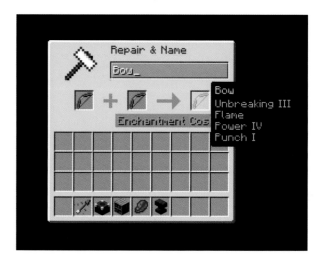

Chapter 9: Enchanting and Potions

Aqua Affinity (I)	Helmet only, lets you see better underwater
Bane of Arthropods (V)	Sword or axe, deal more damage to spiders
Blast Protection (IV)	Armor, reduces the damage and knockback you receive from explosions such as TNT and creepers
Channeling (I)	Trident only, during lightning storms lets you strike enemies with lightning bolts
Depth Strider (III)	Boots only, lets you swim quickly underwater
Efficiency (V)	Pickaxe, shovel, axe, shears, increases the speed that you use the tool
Feather Falling (IV)	Boots only, reduces fall damage
Fire Aspect (II)	Sword only, sets enemies on fire when you hit them
Fire Protection (IV)	Armor, reduces the damage you take from fire
Flame (I)	Bow only, arrows set targets on fire
Fortune (III)	Pickaxe, shovel, axe, increases the probability of getting multiple items from using tools
Frost Walker (II)	Boots only, freezes the water below you, allowing you to walk on its frozen surface
Impaling (V)	Trident only, deal more damage to ocean-dwelling mobs
Infinity (I)	Bow only, provides infinite arrows provided you have at least one in your inventory
Knockback (II)	Sword only, increases the amount your attacks knock enemies backward
Looting (III)	Sword only, increases the amount of loot that mobs drop
Loyalty (III)	Trident only, the trident boomerangs back to you after throwing it
Luck of the Sea (III)	Fishing rod only, increases the chance of getting good items while fishing
Lure (III)	Fishing rod only, decreases the amount of time between bites while fishing
Mending (I)	All items, uses XP to repair durability **NOTE:** *This item is currently only available as a book acquired by trading with librarian villagers or fishing*
Multishot (I)	Crossbow only, fire three arrows at a time while only consuming one
Piercing (IV)	Crossbow only, arrows can fire through multiple mobs
Power (V)	Bow only, increases arrow damage
Projectile Protection (IV)	Armor, reduces damage from enemy projectiles
Protection (IV)	Armor, general purpose damage reduction, though less powerful than damage-specific enchants
Punch (II)	Bow only, increases arrow knockback
Quick Charge (III)	Crossbow, decreases the time it takes to charge shots
Respiration (III)	Helmet only, increases the amount of time you can stay underwater without air
Riptide (III)	Trident only, hurl yourself with your trident in the water or while it's raining
Sharpness (V)	Sword or axe, increases your weapon's damage
Silk Touch (I)	Pickax, shovel, axe, mined blocks remain intact and can be picked up
Smite (V)	Sword or axe, increased damage against undead enemies
Sweeping Edge (III)	Sword only, more damage for sweeping attacks **NOTE:** *Java edition only*
Thorns (III)	Armor, attackers take damage
Unbreaking (III)	All items, increases durability

Potions

Potions can be must-have items when you're heading out for an extended adventure. These consumables provide temporary effects that can be a godsend in certain situations. Need to go underwater for a treasure hunt? Drink a water-breathing potion. Tired of walking into walls when the sun goes down? Take a swig of the night-vision potion and watch the night light up. Brewing can also be expensive, but the potential power that it offers is more than worth the effort.

You can't just whip up potions at will. First, you'll need to build yourself a brewing station. Put it inside your home base, and, to make your life easier, put a water source close by. You'll be using a lot of water in the brewing process, and you'll appreciate not having to run down to the nearest lake or river every time you're ready to brew. Craft some empty glass bottles, and you're ready to start.

The majority of potions start the same way: Put your water-filled bottles in the brewing station and add some nether wart in the top slot. Fuel the station with some blaze powder. Once the brewing process is finished ticking down, you'll have yourself some Awkward Potions. Don't have Nether Wart? It's in the Nether, coincidentally enough, usually found near strongholds. You can grab some of the mushroom-like plants and a little soul sand, and then grow your own little farm back home. You can

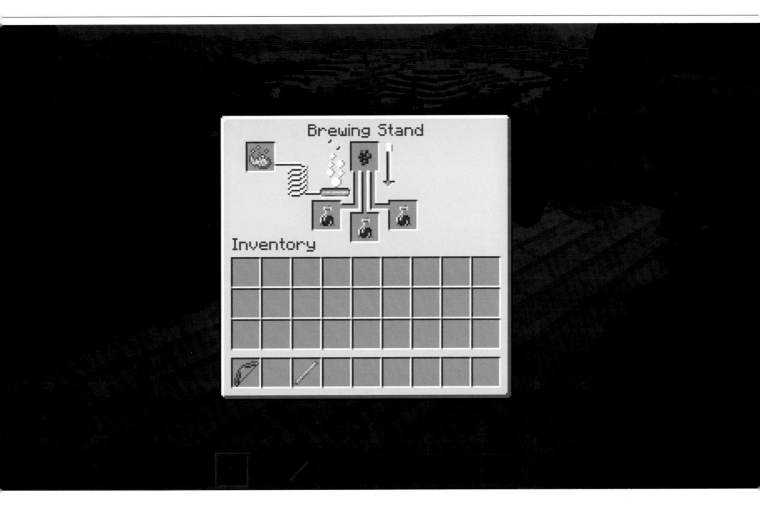

get blaze powder from blaze rods, which can be found by defeating Blazes in the Nether.

Now, you can add another ingredient to your Awkward Potions to get what you're actually looking for, since Awkward Potions don't really do much otherwise. Here's a rundown of what you can add, and what the result will be. Keep in mind that gunpowder, glowstone, and redstone should be added last, and that you can only pick between redstone or glowstone; you can't have potions that are stronger and last longer, unfortunately.

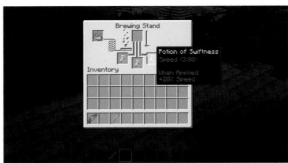

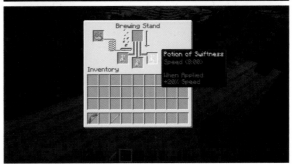

Blaze Powder	Potion of Strength, increases melee damage
Dragon's Breath	Add to completed potion to make a lingering potion that leaves the effect when thrown
Fermented Spider Eye WITHOUT Awkward Potion	Potion of Weakness, reduces melee damage and cures zombie villagers
Ghast Tear	Potion of Regeneration, heals over time
Glistering Melon Slice	Potion of Healing, heals instantly
Glistering Melon Slice THEN Fermented Spider Eye	Potion of Harming, causes damage
Glowstone	Add to completed potion to make potion effects stronge
Golden Carrot	Potion of Night Vision, allows you to see better in the dark
Gunpowder	Add to completed potion to make a splash potion that affects a target when thrown
Magma Cream	Potion of Fire Resistance, negates fire damage
Phantom Membrane	Potion of Slow Falling, slows your fall speed and reduces damage when you land
Puffer Fish	Potion of Water Breathing, allows you to breathe underwater
Redstone	Add to completed potion to make potion effects last longer
Spider Eye	Potion of Poison, causes damage over time
Sugar	Potion of Swiftness, makes the user run faster
Sugar THEN Fermented Spider Eye	Potion of Slowness, makes the user move slower
Turtle Shell	Potion of Turtle Master, reduces user's speed while increasing their overall damage resistance

Areas like this dark forest are much easier to navigate after consuming a night-vision potion.

Minigames, Add-ons, and Other Resources

There's a reason the term "vanilla" is used to describe Minecraft; to many players, the base game is a great start, but it's not complete until all the toppings have been piled onto it. Mods and other add-ons can breathe new life into the ordinary Minecraft experience, add quality-of-life improvements to address a variety of issues, or simply make the game look better than you may have thought possible. Additionally, there are loads of other resources to help you get the most from your Minecraft experience.

Note: The modding scene is much more vibrant on Java, and as such we'll be focusing on Java mods in this section.

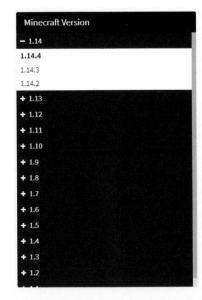

Downloads for Minecraft Forge - MC 1.14.4

All Versions

Note that the downloads in the list below are for getting a *specific* version of Forge. Unless you need this, prefer the links to latest and recommended builds above instead.

Mods Worth Checking Out

Minecraft Forge

First things first. If you're looking for an easy way to get into Minecraft modding on Java, Minecraft Forge should be your initial stop. This is essentially the base mod that many other mods are structured around. Once you download it and apply the file to Minecraft, adding other mods is as simple as putting their .JAR files into the Mods folder on your Minecraft installation.

OptiFine

OptiFine is another must-have. This mod does a lot, not the least of which is allowing you to tweak Minecraft to get the most from your PC. It gives you much more control over a lot of the game's under-the-hood settings, allowing your game to run smoother than ever. As a bonus, OptiFine also makes adding shaders an intuitive and simple process, adding a video-setting option to apply the ones that you've downloaded.

Xaero's Minimap by xaero96

Let's face it: Getting lost stinks. Even if you don't have a tendency to get turned around, being able to get an overhead view of where you're at can be helpful. Can you imagine traveling in an unfamiliar city without GPS? Xaero's Minimap adds a persistent minimap to your screen, highlighting enemies, elevation, and other important information. It might break your immersion a bit if you're fully invested in Minecraft's map-based navigation, but after installing this one don't be surprised if you have a hard time going back.

Break these blocks for a random surprise – which can be positive or negative!

Lucky Block by PlayerInDistress

Ask yourself: Do you feel lucky? If you do, install this popular mod and give it a test. Lucky Block adds breakable question-mark blocks across the world, which will unleash a surprise when broken. Some are good, like getting free resources or unusual potions. Others aren't – how did those angry mobs fit into that tiny package?! Regardless of what lady luck grants you, this mod gives you something fun to look forward to encountering while still retaining the overall Minecraft vibe.

Torchmaster by xalcon

When a regular torch isn't enough, you need something bigger. Torchmaster adds mega torches and other configurable light sources that protect you from mob spawns. These provide much larger areas of safety than traditional torches, allowing you to efficiently light up a village or cave so you can get back to the good stuff. It also lets you build a lamp that prevents passive mobs from spawning, which is handy when you want to be completely isolated.

These last two are small quality-of-life tweaks that may enhance the way you play Minecraft but don't really offer anything interesting from a pure aesthetic perspective.

Friendly Fire by DarkhaxDev

Have you ever entered into a battle frenzy? Or have you had a perfect arrow shot get intercepted by a wandering buddy? Friendly Fire prevents you from accidentally damaging allies, like pets, during combat. Things can get pretty hairy out there; if you find yourself inadvertently turning man's best friend into a pincushion during a bow battle, this mod is worth a look.

Controllable by MrCrayfish

Bedrock players can choose either touchscreen, gamepad, or keyboard and mouse inputs, depending on what platform they're playing on. The Java experience is a little trickier. Getting a gamepad up and running is possible, but it's certainly not a plug-and-play situation. This mod makes it easier, so if you pine for a controller there's really not a good reason to go through the hassle of manually configuring everything. This has you covered.

Shaders Galore!

Shaders are the easiest way to visually overhaul your Minecraft world. They enhance textures, modify the lighting, and basically make everything look much more realistic. If you're a purist, you probably want to steer clear. Everyone else should at least give these a shot. Every creator has their own idea of what looks good, so you'll probably want to experiment to find the one you like best. Fortunately, OptiFine makes swapping between shaders quite simple on Java.

Beyondbelief by Daniel Rodriguez Moya

BSL by Bitslablab

Chocapic13 by Chocapic 13

Continuum by Continuum Graphics

Kuda Shaders by Dedelner

SEUS Renewed by Sonic Ether

Sildur's Vibrant by Sildur

Vanilla Plus Shader by RRe36

These shaders are all for Java, but Bedrock players have something special to look forward to – provided they have the right gear. Graphics-card manufacturer NVIDIA and Mojang are working on a free update that will give owners of high-end NVIDIA cards the ability to play with ray-tracing support. Basically, that means those players will be able to enjoy realistic lighting with reflections, refractive water, and more, that's a step above what's possible with even the best shaders currently out there.

TNT TAG
Round #1

Explosion in 49s

Goal: Tag someone

Alive: 30 Players

11/20/19
www.hypixel.net

You did NOT start as IT! Run away!

Adorkabley is IT!
Cnxiqo_0 is IT!
JasonWong13 is IT!
MinTFoXX is IT!
Universe_Potato is IT!
uM_TeaGod_PvP tagged you!
Cnxiqo_0 is IT!

You're IT, tag someone!

Minigames Worth Your Time

One of the reasons behind Minecraft's longevity is that it's home to a ton of fun multiplayer games. If you haven't dived into that aspect of the game, you should know that these are a significant departure from what you might be familiar with from the single-player experience. In most of these, mining and exploration take a backseat to more pressing matters, like staying alive.

When you hop into a multiplayer server or Realm for the first time, it's understandable if you're overwhelmed with all the options. With that in mind, here are some solid picks for you to explore. The best part is that if one of these modes doesn't click with you for whatever reason, there's always something different to try. These are all great places to start.

Hide and Seek

This is blocky spin on a familiar childhood game. The twist is that the hiders (picked randomly at the start of each round) are camouflaged. When

In the image overlay:

BED WARS
11/20/19 m422H
Diamond II in 5:49

R Red: ✓
B Blue: ✓
G Green: ✓
Y Yellow: ✓
A Aqua: ✓
W White: ✓ YOU
P Pink: ✓
S Gray: ✓

www.hypixel.net

] [YELLOW] theuncommengamer dc olan varmi

a round starts, hiders can pick what object they'd like to take the form of – things like, steps, crates, and other mundane objects. They then have a limited amount of time to run around the level and find a place to hide. When they stand still for a few moments, their character "clicks" into place, aligning on the Minecraft grid to better blend in. The seekers then run around and bonk everything that looks suspicious. Does that hay bale look out of place in that otherwise empty hallway? Rounds are fast, and there's a frantic thrill that comes with popping out of hiding just after a seeker passes by as you try to find an even better hiding spot.

Bed Wars

Bed Wars is one of the bigger games in Minecraft, and for good reason: It's really, really fun. Players have two main tasks to prioritize after spawning in their world: keeping their bed safe while also working to destroy the other players' beds. You can engage with other players by bridging out to their island bases, but they'll keep coming back until you blow up their beds. Your base constantly generates materials, which you can use to upgrade your gear and build traps to keep interlopers at bay.

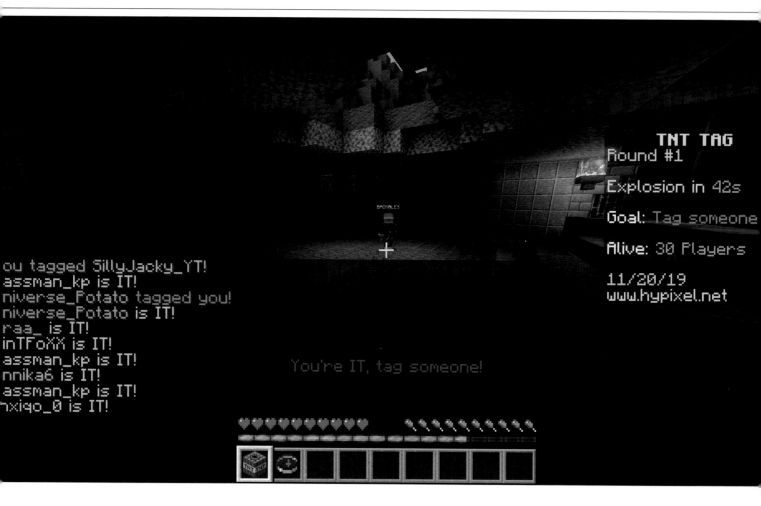

TNT TAG
Round #1

Explosion in 42s

Goal: Tag someone

Alive: 30 Players

11/20/19
www.hypixel.net

ou tagged SillyJacky_YT!
assman_kp is IT!
niverse_Potato tagged you!
niverse_Potato is IT!
raa_ is IT!
inTFoXX is IT!
assman_kp is IT!
nnika6 is IT!
assman_kp is IT!
hxiqo_0 is IT!

You're IT, tag someone!

TNT Tag

This is about as simple as it gets, but that doesn't make it any less fun. TNT Tag starts with a group of players, with several of them designated "it," which is visually represented with a bundle of TNT balanced on their avatar's head. Yikes! Those players need to tag other players to transfer the status before the bomb explodes. There are tag-backs, so make sure you make a hasty retreat if you manage to pass along the explosive. Each round ends with a bang – and hopefully you aren't the source of one of those craters.

Murder Mystery

Murder Mystery is like a hybrid of tag and hide-and-seek. At the start of each round, one player is chosen randomly to be the murderer, and another is the sheriff. Everyone else is just a potential

victim. The murderer and sheriff are both armed, but everyone else is helpless. The goal changes, depending on your role. As murderer, you need to eliminate all the other players. The sheriff is the only player who can get rid of the murderer. The game ends when all the players are dead or the murderer is eliminated. An Assassin variant gives each player a specific target. Your job is to look at your contract and get the person whose picture appears on it. Be careful though, since you're on someone else's sheet, too.

Skywars

Skywars is similar to Bed Wars, only it has more of a straight-up combat focus. Think of it as The Hunger Games set on floating islands. Players start off in glass capsules, suspended over their little chunk of land. After breaking free, they land on their hub island. Chests are filled with armor, weapons, and other essentials, but the good stuff is typically located in the main center island. Unsurprisingly, that's where most of the action usually ends up taking place.

Other Resources

If you have a question about Minecraft – and you're inevitably going to have a question about Minecraft – there are plenty of places to find the answers. Here are a few additional resources that will help steer you toward the right direction.

Official Minecraft Wiki (Minecraft.gamepedia.com)

This is the big one. Minecraft has a phenomenal community, as evidenced by this comprehensive resource. If you have any questions about a specific game mechanic, mob, or material, odds are this wiki will have the answers.

All screenshots for criticism and review. Minecraft®™ & © 2009-2020 Mojang

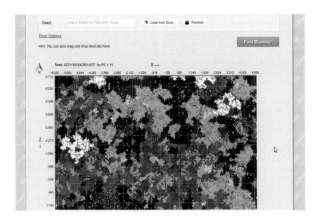

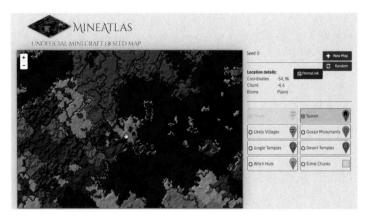

Biome Finder (chunkbase.com) and Mine Atlas (mineatlas.com)

Exploration is a key part of Minecraft – or it can be, if you're into that. Sometimes you might just want to head in a direction with a destination in mind. That can be difficult in a new Minecraft spawn, when your map is basically a giant question mark. Both Biome Finder and Mine Atlas are sites that you can put your Minecraft seed into to learn more about your surroundings. They show off biomes and points of interest, and you can scroll around the world and get a better sense of what's around you. They may not be completely in tune with your current version of the game, but even so the overall placement of biomes should be close enough to give you a broad heads up on where you need to head.

Minecraft Seed HQ (minecraftseedhq.com)

Are you in the mood to fight a witch? Maybe you want to see what life's like in the arctic? Or is a mesa more your style? Minecraft Seed HQ has a constantly updated list of great seeds that are tailored to whatever kind of world you want to be in. Colorful maps and other tips provide guidance for players who are interested in trying out new worlds but not necessarily going into them completely blind. Getting a dud world is always a bummer, and Minecraft Seed HQ's community-driven contributions can help steer you toward something good.

It doesn't get much more obvious than this, but YouTube is one of the all-time best places to go for all things Minecraft. Someone else has probably already done just about anything you can think of, particularly if you're just starting out your Minecraft career. Stuck on a redstone contraption? Looking for a fun house design? Or do you just want to be entertained? There are a wide variety of great YouTubers putting out high-quality content, like DanTDM, Pixlriffs, Wattles, and more.

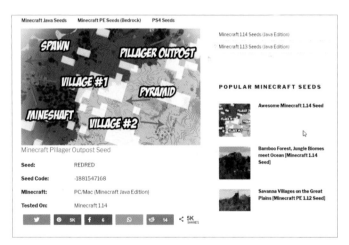

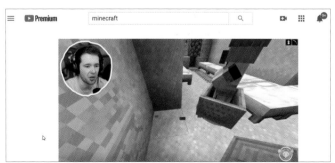

Minecraft Earth and Minecraft Dungeons

Minecraft fans have another way to engage with the game and all its blocky trimmings. Better still, players can do it while getting to know the actual world around them. Minecraft Earth is an augmented-reality game, which adds a layer of gameplay and interactivity to real-world locations. If you're familiar with Pokémon Go, you know exactly what we're talking about. All you need is a supported Android or iOS device and the desire to go out and explore.

Chapter 11: Minecraft Earth

In this chapter, we'll share everything you need to know to make the most of your Minecraft Earth experience, and also highlight another place you can go to get your Minecraft fix. Let's go!

If you've never dabbled with other AR games, let's get you up to speed quickly. These games tap into your mobile device's GPS and display a map of the world around you. When you first start these games, it looks as though you're using a navigational tool. The difference is that you're able to interact with locations around you, once you get within their range. Those interactions are typically enhanced by tapping into your phone's camera, further enhancing the illusion that Pokémon, dinosaurs, or whatever is thematically appropriate are wandering around the world around you – invisible to anyone who isn't playing the game.

Minecraft Earth takes that core idea and adds what's arguably the meatiest chunk of gameplay that the genre has seen. You're not just walking around and tapping points of interest – though that's certainly a component of the game. The items that you collect during your travels can be used in actual Minecraft constructions, which can then be "placed" in the world around you. Instead of passively looking at the things that the game's creators have built, Minecraft Earth players can design their own houses and other structures, and then interact with those in much the same way they do in mainline Minecraft. And better yet, they can do so with friends. After all, Minecraft is perhaps best enjoyed with a buddy.

Before we go much further, it's important to note that Minecraft Earth is still early in its lifespan, and some elements that we discuss could be changing as features mature and others are added. The core concepts should remain relevant, however.

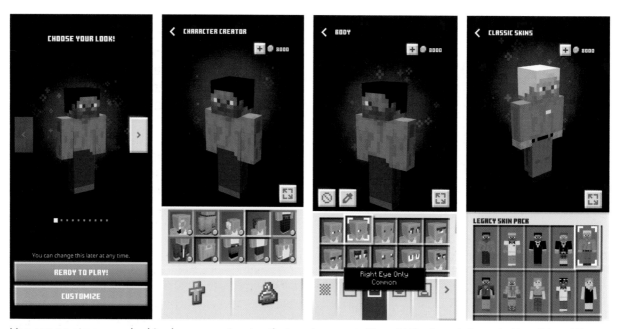

You can create premade skins here or customize their various parts if you'd like to get down to the nitty gritty.

The Basics

When you start Minecraft Earth for the first time, you'll be prompted to enter your Microsoft login. Bedrock players have an advantage here, since that's the same account that's used to access that version of the game. If you're a Java player, you may have to create one – if you don't already have one from using Xbox Live or one of Microsoft's other services.

After that, you'll enter the skin-selection part of the game. There are a variety of different presets to choose from, or you can dive into the character-creation section to create your own unique character. Once again, Bedrock players will get a little extra something in Minecraft Earth. If you play on that version and have purchased or unlocked other skins, you'll be able to access them all here, too. Additionally, some of the cosmetic options can be purchased using your Minecraft coins. Don't feel as though you need to spend a single dime here, if you don't want to; as with normal Minecraft, skins are purely cosmetic and don't have any bearing on the actual game. If you want to immediately pick Minecraft Steve and move along, there's no reason

to linger if the idea of playing dress-up doesn't appeal to you.

Once you've chosen your character skin, you'll pop into the world. Don't panic if you regret your decision – you can enter the character-customization screen again at any time by tapping on your player icon in the upper-left corner and selecting the "characters" option. Your character should be standing in the center of a pulsing circle. That circle represents the zone that you're able to interact with at any given moment. If you turn your device around, the map should spin with you, highlighting some of the other places you can visit in the distance.

There are actually two different ways you can navigate in the world. If you see a little icon superimposed on the compass in the upper-right of the screen, that means that the game will orient itself to align with whatever way you're facing. If you're looking north, your character will point in the same direction. You can either tap the compass icon or drag your finger along the screen to check out the other navigation option. In this mode, you manually fix the orientation to whatever way you

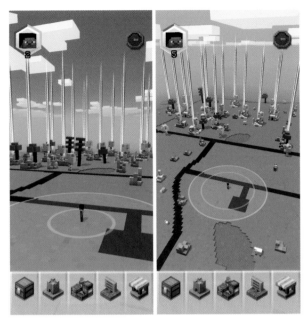

Pulling back and rotating your view can give you a better idea of which way you should explore.

common way to interact with Minecraft Earth. Nearly every time you start the game, you'll be surrounded by them – and odds are, some will be within your immediate range. So what are these things? Basically, Tappables are collectibles that add items to your inventory. You can't really mine in Minecraft Earth, but that doesn't mean that foraging for materials isn't part of the experience. When you tap on a Tappable, you'll see a quick transitional screen, where you're prompted to keep tapping on the object to reveal what exactly it holds. After a few moments of buildup, the item will explode and reveal its contents. Ta-dah!

If you take a quick look around the map around you, you'll see all kinds of trees, rock structures, and mounds of dirt. They're all Tappables, even though they look different. The contents may be a surprise, but the form that each Tappable takes will provide a general sense of what you can expect

want. This is an easier way to get your bearings, when you're not in the mood to spin around. We typically shift between both modes while we play, but ultimately this is another case where how you proceed is entirely up to you. If you'd like a better vantage point, you can also put two fingers on your screen and move them apart to zoom out of the map, or pinch them together to zoom back in.

All right! Now that you know how to get around, it's time to talk Tappables. Tappables are the most

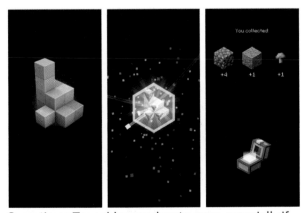

Sometimes Tappables are slow to open, especially if your connection is poor. Be patient!

Power Play

Minecraft Earth is a lot of fun, but you'll pay for it in battery life. The game is a tremendous power hog, capable of draining a fully charged device to half power in less than an hour. As you might imagine, that can be a problem. For that reason, if you plan on playing for more than a few minutes at a time, we recommend purchasing an external battery pack. These devices attach to your phone or tablet and will either act as a larger battery reserve or allow you to charge a dwindling device when you aren't near an outlet.

They range in price from about $30 to $100, and will let you play significantly longer than you would otherwise. There are too many on the market to call out individually, but some good brands to look out for are Anker, Belkin, and Jackery.

to get from them. For instance, tree Tappables will typically provide wood, while stone structures will give you several blocks of stone. There aren't any hostile mobs wandering around in Minecraft Earth – at least, not yet – but you will spy chickens, cows, sheep, and pigs. They're still Tappables, even though they have at least one special property that sets them apart.

Animal mobs will move around on the map a little bit. They're not going to wander far, but they'll walk enough to remind you that they are indeed animals. You can use that to your benefit if you see one spawning just outside your character's circle. If you're patient, there's a chance that they'll walk into your range, where you can then tap and collect them like any other Tappable. It's not a huge deal, but it can save you a little walking if you're feeling

lazy. Animals will be added to your inventory the same way as other items. It should be noted that Minecraft Earth adds a few new mobs to look out for, including the Cluckshroom (a chicken version of Minecraft's red, mushroom-covered Mooshroom), a dirty flower-covered pig, and some others. They're rare, so don't be disappointed if you don't immediately find them. Some animals will give you additional materials, like feathers. All will give you a little bit of experience when you collect them, which is universal across Tappables.

Chests can also appear as Tappables, and these often contain some of the harder-to-find items. Blocks and materials are pretty easy to collect, but things like redstone, TNT blocks, and note blocks aren't as commonplace. Chests generally have higher-quality stuff, so it makes sense to go out of

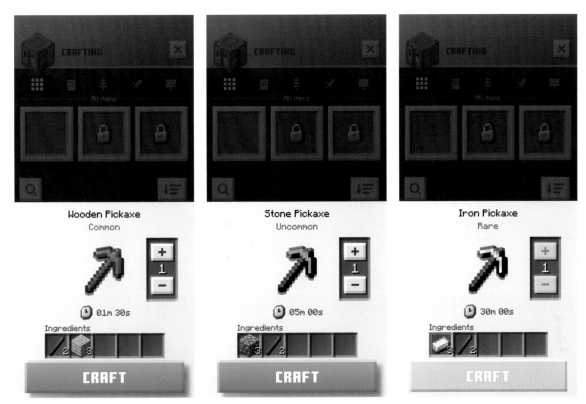

The higher an item's quality, the longer it will take to craft. It's best to keep things going in the background so you aren't stuck waiting when you want to play.

your way to collect them when you can. Overall, items are ranked in rarity, from common (white), uncommon (green), rare (blue), and epic (purple).

Once you've collected a few items, you should pay a quick visit to your inventory and admire your collection. You can do that by tapping on the chest icon on the bottom-left side of the screen. Here, you can sort it in the ways you'd expect, by rarity, alphabetically, and by quantity. You can also cycle through item categories, such as mobs, construction, nature, equipment, and items. Chances are, you're going to come up noticeably short on the equipment tab. You don't need any gear to interact with Tappables; you can think about those as "punching trees" kind of encounters. You're going to need some items before we engage with the next part of Minecraft Earth, so back out of the inventory and click on the "make stuff" tab, which is the icon in the middle of the bottom toolbar.

You don't need to worry about building crafting tables or smelters in Minecraft Earth. You'll still have to put in your time if you want to gear up. Like a lot of other mobile games, time is actually one of the biggest resources in the game. Click on the empty slot in the crafting section, and you'll see what items you can make from your recipe book. Like your inventory, you can check out various categories, including equipment. Go here, and see what you need to build a pickaxe. As with regular Minecraft, try to see if you can build a stone one first, because it'll last longer than a wooden one. You'll need sticks and either stone or wooden planks to build it. If you don't have enough materials, you'll have to do some exploring to get the required components from Tappables. We'll wait.

Before you head out the door, you should know one thing about Tappables: They refresh over time. If you need to collect a lot of items, or if you're just eager to explore the neighborhood, by all means, be our guests. If you only need a few things or don't want to head out (or can't, for whatever reason), don't worry. New Tappables will cycle into the world after a little while (around seven minutes or so, at our last count), with some of those usually appearing within your immediate vicinity. Keep an eye out for animals that plop into the world, because their spawning animations are kind of funny.

All right! Once you have the materials for your pickaxe, go ahead and build it. You'll notice that a timer will start after you begin the construction process. Now you just need to wait. You can queue up multiples of the same items, but until you unlock additional crafting slots, you can only have one item going at a time. After you make your pickaxe, make a sword. Once that's completed, you're ready for the next big part of the game: adventures!

Adventure Time!

Tappables aren't the only points of interest that appear on the game map. Adventures are the second big element to Minecraft Earth, and they're represented by blocky structures that are slightly larger than Tappable formations. To make it even easier, these are the things that have beacon-like pillars of light emitting from them. Adventures function much differently than Tappables, which is why you need to be prepared before engaging with them.

Let's face it: Tappables are on the low end of the interactivity scale. They're technically something that you play with, but aside from the immediate rush of surprise that comes with opening them up, there isn't a whole lot there. Adventures are much meatier in the gameplay department, and they're a step closer to what you might expect to get from a Minecraft AR game.

Adventures are more range dependent than Tappables, meaning that you have to get pretty close to them before you can do anything with them. Even if they're within your circular field, there's a good chance that you'll have to do some

additional walking to line things up properly. You'll know that you're set when the Adventure's outline isn't red, and when the "Play" button is highlighted. Once you hit that button, you may get a prompt telling you that your toolbar is empty. Be sure to go into your inventory and add your pickaxe, sword, and whatever else you want to bring with you. You only have nine slots, but that should be plenty for the vast majority of your adventuring.

Chapter 11: Minecraft Earth

Unlike Tappables, you have to do a little extra legwork before you can begin. That means that you have to "place" the Adventure into the world around you. If you've poked around with the game's buildplates, you already understand this step. If not, we'll get to that in a little while. At this point, you'll see the world around you via your devices camera, along with an overlay where you can put

This is a bad place to put an adventure, unless you are a fish.

the Adventure. Once you find a suitable spot, place it, and you're ready to go.

This part is important, so don't just drop it wherever. You may have to do some walking around in the Adventure, so try to find a spot that gives you some room to maneuver. This seems like a no-brainer, but don't put it down in the middle of a puddle or in a cluster of thorns, unless you want to get wet or poked. Minecraft Earth does its best to not put Adventures near areas like major roads or busy thoroughfares, but ultimate responsibility is up to you. As with other AR games, be respectful of the areas around you, and also be aware and careful about your surroundings!

Whew! Once it's placed you'll then see what it might be like to live in Minecraft. Pretty cool, right? Everything around you will behave the way it does in proper Minecraft, with water flowing from source blocks, lava burning things that fall within its path, and mobs wandering around. It's probably a good idea to play these with the sound on, because there's a good chance that you might run into some hostile mobs on your Adventure, even if you can't see them.

Your main objective in Adventures is to gather as many resources as you can. Unlike Tappables, you can actually see what you're going to get. Mine some dirt or iron ore, and you'll receive dirt and iron ore. If you bring tools like buckets along, you can use them to get water and lava. Bedrock is much

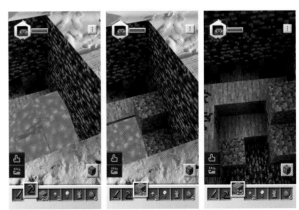

It's a good idea to block lava sources when you can, so you can get to the resources that are being covered. Who knows what you'll find?

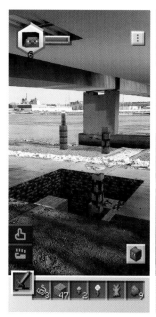

Combat works similarly to Minecraft's, though you may experience an added sense of immediacy to it all. Somehow, a skeleton's arrows seem much more dangerous when they appear to be whizzing by your actual head. You can avoid projectiles by leaning out of the way before they hit. If you're getting attacked and don't know where it's coming from, an indicator on the side of the screen should point you toward the threat. Swords have the same magically lengthened range as their mining contemporaries in Minecraft Earth, so swing at any targets you see – no matter how far they might be from you.

You can take damage from hostile mobs, so it might not be a bad idea to bring some food along with you. Weapons and tools will lose durability after using them, so it's possible that you might break them. In either event, don't worry – you can leave the Adventure, regroup, and then continue where you left off. Adventures have a finite time limit once you place them, but it's generous enough to allow you to drop in and out at least once without losing all of your progress. Once you've gathered enough materials, slain your share of mobs, and seen everything you think you need to see, head out for good. You'll get the supplies you've found and whatever experience you've earned.

closer to the surface here, so don't be alarmed if you strike that. The worlds that Adventures create are box shaped, lined with the indestructible material. Everything else is fair game, so have at it.

Since the game is layered onto our reality, the rules are slightly different. There's a really great effect you can experience by looking down into the Adventure, where you might peer down into a mysterious dark chasm. It's pretty convincing, but (obviously) it's just an illusion. Nothing is going to happen if you step onto the playing field, aside from the game acting a bit strange. In short, don't worry; you're not going to fall into the world, so feel free to maneuver around to better get a sense of the Adventure around you and what kind of mining opportunities are there.

Another big change from regular Minecraft is that you don't have to be near anything to mine it or collect resources. If you can see a mineable block, your tools will reach it. If you kill a skeleton or other mob, the resources it drops can be gathered by tapping them – no matter how far away they might be. It makes life a lot easier, and cuts down on the amount of real-world maneuvering you might otherwise have to do.

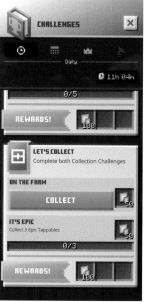

Adventures can be easily shared with other players. All you have to do is tap into an Adventure to get playing, whether it's alone or with people who have already started it. All materials are shared, so you don't have to worry about any "Who picked up that diamond?" kind of drama. Other players will have their usernames highlighted on them when they appear on your screen, and you can also see what tool or item they're holding in their hands.

Building In New Ways

All right! You've collected some Tappables and gone on a few Adventures. Your inventory is packed with blocks and other goodies. What are you supposed to do with all this stuff? It should come as no surprise that the final major part of Minecraft Earth focuses on building and user-created construction.

The second icon on the main screen's toolbar will bring you to the buildplates section. This is where you'll be able to express your creativity, or just explore some of the things that Microsoft and Mojang have created. When you first start Minecraft Earth, you'll have access to one 8x8 block plate. It's a nice place to begin, but if you scroll down you'll see that it's only the beginning. As you level up in the game, you'll have access to additional buildplates. Like a lot of other mobile games out there, there's also a store where you can purchase additional ones. It's worth clicking the store button in the buildplates section at least once, even if you don't plan on ever spending any money on the game.

The store has even more buildplates for sale, which can be purchased using rubies, Minecraft Earth's premium currency. You can buy ruby bundles, but you also earn them randomly from Tappables. If you enjoy the building component of the game, it might not be a bad idea to hoard your rubies until you're able to purchase one of the larger 16x16 buildplates to give you more options in the future.

Buildplates and Adventures have a similar real-world component tied to them, so you'll need to place them before you can interact with them. Before you do anything with your buildplate, you'll notice that you have a couple of options in the buildplate-selection screen. If you select build, you'll place a small, model-size version of the plate onto your floor, table, or other suitable work surface. The "play" button will let you drop a life-sized version of your creation into the world, using the same scale as the models in Adventures. You'll definitely need more room for these builds. There are a few other important differences to be aware of, which we'll explore more in depth shortly.

Buildplates have a default build on them, but don't feel bad about breaking it. Minecraft is about creation, and you may want to start with a fresh slate. Or, if you like the look of the starter build but just want to make some tweaks, feel free to go that route, too.

Building is fairly self-explanatory, but we'll go over a few highlights. The menu button in the upper right will let you activate what they call "precision mode." This puts a targeting reticle on your screen, which might be handy if you're looking to be, well, more precise with your block placement. The hand and chest icons on the bottom left toggle between interact and pickup modes, respectively. Interact mode lets you do things like opening gates or flipping switches, while pickup mode will break the blocks you select and return them to your inventory. You can walk around your build to get a better view, or you can touch and drag the screen to manually rotate it – which is particularly handy if you're building on a desk that's placed against a wall or is otherwise difficult to walk around. Be sure to touch the floor or other non-build part if you want to do that, so you don't accidentally break or remove any blocks from your creation.

You only have the blocks you have in Minecraft Earth, so if you need more wood for your dream

house you may have to hit the trail and find it. Or, you can enlist the help of a friend or two. Building is better with friends, after all. Multiplayer is a great way to play Minecraft Earth, but it comes with some of the biggest "BEWARE" signs that the game has to offer. As in traditional Minecraft, the potential for mischief is very real in Minecraft Earth's multiplayer, so only invite people you trust.

To let your friends play with you, hit the menu button in the upper right and select "Invite friend." Strange, right? Your device will then show a screen with a QR code on it, which they can scan using their device. The code-scanning part can be accessed from the signpost icon in the toolbar, from the main game. There, they'll see an option named "Join friend." At that point, they just need to center your device on their screen and the rest will happen automatically.

Ta-dah! You're playing together! Your experience will be different depending on what mode you (or the host) is playing on. If you're in build mode, which is the one that uses the smaller model-like setup, players can build things using whatever they have in their inventories. The opposite also holds; users can break blocks, and those materials will be added to their inventories. It's great if you're playing with people you trust, but you can see how things might get out of hand if another player

You may be able to get larger builds in your house, but the 16x16 plates are probably best experienced in the open air.

decided they wanted to wreak havoc on your world. If you're not sure where your fellow players fall on the good/evil alignment charts, there's a safer way to play together.

The life-sized buildplate models don't retain changes, meaning that they're the safest way to show off your creations without risking any permanent damage to them. It's also a super fun way to share what you've made. Your less-than-trustworthy buddies can peer through your virtual home's windows, but you don't need to worry about them smashing the glass. And even if you do trust your building companions, seeing your handiwork at this scale is impressive.

Minecraft's wild, imaginative worlds have always called to us, and it's easy to imagine what it might be like to be teleported into the game. Minecraft Earth gets us about as close to that fantasy as we'd like. Once you see a Creeper in Adventure-mode scale, you'll probably agree that they probably don't have any business walking around with the rest of us.

Don't Tap and Drive!

You have to do a fair bit of walking if you want to collect resources through Tappables. If you think that you've devised a workaround, hold up – you can't play Minecraft Earth efficiently while driving. The game can detect when you're traveling at higher-than-walking rates of speed, and it disables much of its functionality at that point. You'll be able to see your character cruising around in a minecart, but you won't be able to interact with any of the game's elements. Control is handed back over once you hit a more suitable speed. In other words, you can't game the system, even if you're a passenger and someone else is doing the driving.

LOCATE VILLAGERS
LEFT BEHIND

MINECRAFT DUNGEONS

Pack your torches, weapons, and sense of adventure in this dungeon-crawling Minecraft spinoff.

Wow! Mojang's been busy these past few years. In addition to keeping Minecraft updated and helping to deliver Minecraft Earth, a small team within the studio has designed an all-new Minecraft spinoff that pushes combat and exploration to the forefront. Minecraft Dungeons is an action-RPG that lets a party of up to four adventurers team up against a

host of new and familiar foes, while gathering loads of loot in the process. The ultimate goal? To find and defeat the evil Arch-Illager, a powerful foe who has been corrupted by the Orb of Dominance.

If you manage to rally four friends together, the odds are good that at least one of you is familiar with the core concepts behind the dungeon-crawling genre. If not, don't worry! These games have been around for decades on PC, with Blizzard's Diablo series being an early and important touchstone. The core gameplay focuses on exploring dangerous lands, fighting monsters, and gaining more and more powerful loot. The loot component is particularly important to the genre. As you get better weapons and armor, you're able to delve deeper into the world, which, as you might expect, probably contains more dungeons than what you encounter on your day-to-day travels.

Minecraft Dungeons shares a lot of those elements, but has its own fairly unique takes here and there. Most notably, it takes full advantage of its relation to the Minecraft series. We're all familiar with Minecraft's mobs, and they're all represented in Dungeons. Experienced Minecrafters will start off with a great advantage, since they'll immediately know what to do when you see a Creeper (back off!) or know that an odd, skittering sound from offscreen means that a cave spider is waiting for an ambush.

Gear is a big part of the game, but it's handled a bit differently from many other dungeon-crawlers. Most notably, there aren't any level requirements associated with items. If you find a new piece of armor or tasty-looking weapon, you can immediately start using it. Your character will gain experience and levels as you kill mobs and explore, but those levels work the same way as they do in Minecraft. They don't change any inherent qualities with your hero, such as how much health they have or their innate damage output, but levels can be spent on enchantments, which in turn will let you make your gear better. What this means for players is that even completely new adventurers aren't at

a huge disadvantage when they group up with their experienced friends. Once they pick up a few pieces of gear, they'll be able to mix it up with the rest of the crew – no catching up required.

That sense of playful freedom extends to the way that roles and classes are handled. In essence, they're not a permanent part of Minecraft Dungeons. Just as players don't have any roles in Minecraft, they don't have to align themselves to any particular style of play in Dungeons. If you want to be a melee-focused brawler, equip axes and thicker armor. Prefer to hang back and blast skeletons and other monsters with spells? Put on mage gear and you're set. Artifacts and totems have a similar flexibility. If you want to be a healer, put a healing totem in your hotbar and help keep your team alive – even if you're playing as a barbarian-style hero. You can change your gear and loadouts at will.

Players will have plenty to discover on their own, but here are a few helpful tips to make your early moments a bit easier:

- **Keep an eye out for enemies lurking in the sidelines.** It's easy to get distracted by the immediate threats that are in your face, but the bad guys that hang out a bit away from the action can be just as deadly. For instance, we all know what it's like to get picked off by a skeleton archer in Minecraft when you're busy doing something else. Some enemies in Dungeons are built around being pests. If you spy an Enchanter in the field of combat, prioritize him. These book-wielding baddies can give their friends special buffs, which in turn can make your life particularly difficult. Get rid of them as soon as you can, and the other mobs will be easier.

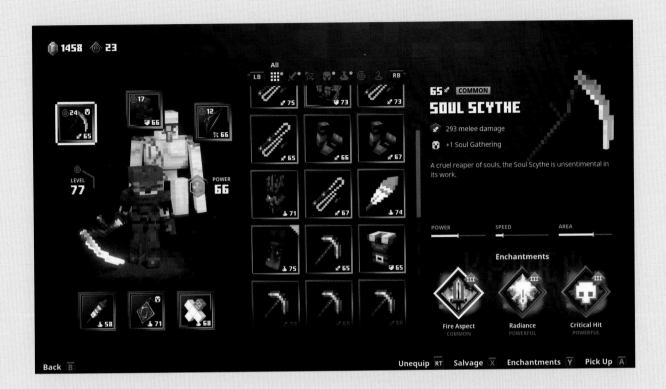

Four players can team up, either via couch-style co-op or online. The difficulty will scale as you add more players, so be careful. There's always a temptation to split up and do your own thing (something that's easier when you're not sharing a screen in local co-op), but doing so comes with risks. If you get too far from the party and meet your end, you'll have to wait for a revive. Players have an added incentive to work together, because if a player isn't revived quickly enough, night will fall – which brings waves of even tougher enemies.

Enchantments are critically important. For your bow, the Infinite enchant gives you a random chance of firing an arrow at no cost. Snowball enchants can stun and slow approaching enemies, giving you time to best line up your attacks. There aren't any that are complete wastes, but keep your playstyle in mind. If you like taking on enemies with long-range attacks, it might not make sense to use an enchant that bends gravity to pull foes closer.

New items and more powerful gear is unlocked as you beat each of the game's three difficulty levels, so prioritize plowing through the campaign as soon as you can. At first, your gear can only hold one or two enchants per item, but late-game gear can have up to three enchants. It does get harder as you go, so you'll need that kind of powerful equipment if you hope to beat the final Apocalypse difficulty setting. Good luck!

Minecraft Dungeons is available on Nintendo Switch, PC, PlayStation 4, and Xbox One.

Other Games to Try

Minecraft may offer players a staggering amount of freedom and ways to play, but that doesn't mean it's the only way to satisfy the urge to build, farm, or fight. If you enjoy Minecraft but are looking for something a little different, these recommended games cover some of the same territory while providing all-new experiences.

If You Like Minecraft, Try...

No Man's Sky

ESRB Rating: T

Play it on: PC, PlayStation 4, Xbox One

Players who love the thrill of seeing strange new landscapes and surviving in hostile conditions should feel right at home in this massive game. Like Minecraft, the lands of No Man's Sky are randomly built, so you never know exactly what's over the next hill. Hello Games took it several steps further, however, with entire planets, solar systems, and galaxies that are filled with surprises – including the plants and wildlife that populate these often strange locations.

It's been out a few years now, and several major updates have been released since that time. Players have a lot more to do than just hop in their spaceships and travel from planet to planet. If you find a place you want to call home, a fairly deep base-building system allows you to establish roots in a fully customizable home base. More story elements have also been added, giving players who might need a little guidance a push in the right direction.

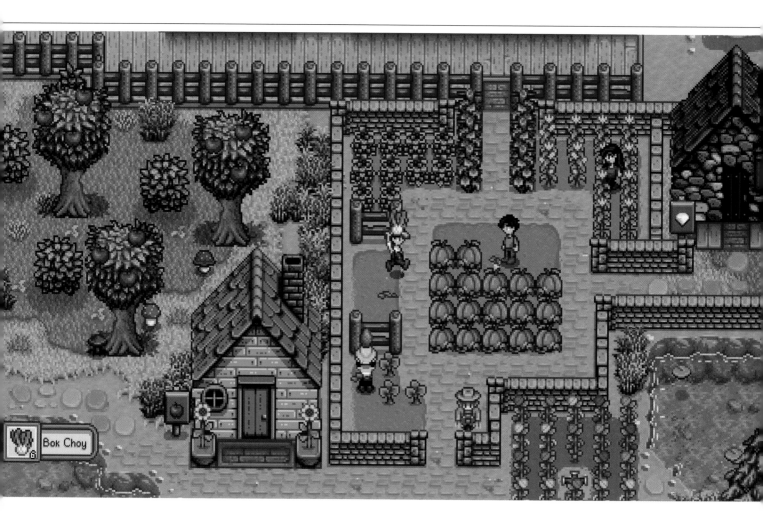

Bok Choy

Stardew Valley

ESRB Rating: E10+

Play it on: Android, iOS, PC, PlayStation 4,

Switch, Vita, Xbox One

Farmers, take note: Stardew Valley is all about your favorite Minecraft pastime. If you get a kick out of planting crops, maintaining your fields, and reaping the rewards – literally – then this is the game for you. Eric Barone's indie sensation drops you into a lovely little town, and challenges your character to bring a neglected patch of land back from the brink.

Farm life isn't just about toiling in the sun, however. There's a healthy dose of social interactivity with the town's NPCs, for players who enjoy hanging out with villagers. Like in Minecraft, you can trade with these folks, but you can also build friendships and even get married. And when you need to get away from it all, there are plenty of mines to explore. That sounds a little familiar, doesn't it?

Dragon Quest Builders 2

ESRB Rating: E10+

Play it on: PlayStation 4, Switch

Dragon Quest Builders 2 is based on Square Enix's long-running RPGs, but don't be alarmed if you aren't up to speed on that series. This spin-off tells an all-new tale and, better still, it's one built around the legend of a talented builder. It's hard to ignore some of the visual similarities between this title and Minecraft, but Builders 2 puts more of an emphasis on story and combat – while still offering plenty of room for self expression.

Unlike a lot of other RPGs, the NPCs aren't afraid to help you out here. They'll maintain your crops and even help with some construction projects, giving you more time to explore and build. Builders 2's community has created some incredible builds, which you can easily visit for inspiration or just for fun. As in Minecraft, you can play cooperatively, but that option requires a fair bit of exploration before it unlocks.

Hytale

ESRB Rating: N/A

Play it on: PC

If you've spent much time exploring Minecraft's multiplayer servers or minigames, chances are you've come across Hypixel Studio's work. The developers aren't content with bringing top-notch content to Minecraft; they're working on their very own game, another open-world sandbox called Hytale. It looks a lot like Mojang's title, but with plenty of features and tools that give Hytale its very own identity.

Like Minecraft, Hytale features procedurally generated worlds and exploration. It's being designed with modding in mind, meaning that players can expect to have access to a ton of fun minigames and mods – and even the ability to watch movies and videos together. The game is currently in beta, which means that features and functionality is still being added. It's worth visiting the official website and signing up for a chance to check it out yourself in the meantime.

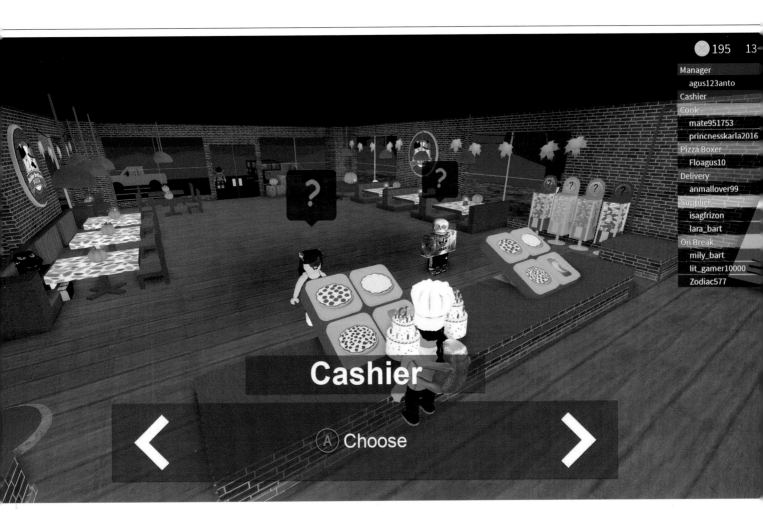

Roblox

ESRB Rating: E10+

Play it on: Android, iOS, PC, PlayStation 4, Xbox One

Poke around the world of user-generated content, and you're bound to see Roblox pop up. It's one of the most popular destinations around, thanks to the fact that it's playable on a wide array of devices and consoles and that it's home to literally thousands of different games. They run the gamut from competitive shooters like Phantom Forces to lifestyle sims like Work at a Pizza Place to thrilling adventures like Natural Disaster Survival.

Not all of the games are worth playing, but you can think of it like interactive channel-surfing. If you don't like what's going on, finding something new is only a few button presses away. You'll undoubtedly have moments where you'll think you could come up with something better, and guess what? Thanks to intuitive tools and a friendly community, you can make your own Roblox experiences if you're feeling ambitious. Who knows? Maybe you can be the next big game designer!

Subnautica

ESRB Rating: E10+

Play it on: PC, PlayStation 4, Xbox One

Do you dig the expanded underwater content that came with Minecraft's Update Aquatic? Unknown Worlds' open-world survival game hits many of the same exploratory notes while offering its own unique adventure. After crash-landing on a mysterious planet, how – or if – you survive is in large part up to you.

There are a lot of dangerous things under the seemingly placid sea, and you'll need to craft survival gear if you want to be able to face it. In addition to the mainline adventure, the developers are working on a chilly sequel called Below Zero. If you enjoyed Subnautica already or would rather go on a journey somewhere a little colder, you can check out the work-in-progress version on PC.

Lego Worlds

ESRB Rating: E10+

Play it on: PC, PlayStation 4, Switch, Xbox One

Minecraft can be reminiscent of playing with a massive box of Lego blocks, so it only seemed fitting that the toy company got in on the fun. Lego Worlds lets you build your own minifig character and let them explore a bunch of procedurally generated worlds. It's developed by many of the same people who made the other Lego video games, so expect plenty of slapstick humor, too.

When you're ready to build – and building is a big part of Lego Worlds – you can do it either by working with preset templates or expressing yourself brick by brick. The tools are intuitive, and because it uses recognizable elements from the iconic toy line, you can easily replicate some of your favorite childhood builds.

If You're Into Minecraft Earth, Try...

Pokémon Go

ESRB Rating: N/A

Play it on: Android, iOS

Pokémon Go was a phenomenon when it came out in 2016, giving players a reason to explore the world around them while collecting monsters. Niantic has been updating it ever since, adding multiplayer raids, trades, and an expanded roster of creatures to populate your Pokédex.

The core gameplay isn't quite as deep or engaging as Minecraft Earth, but the size of its community is a reason to check it out. Getting out and meeting people is one of the big draws of these augmented-reality experiences, and Pokémon Go's continued popularity make it an easy choice if you're looking to get outside and make some new friends.

Harry Potter: Wizards Unite

ESRB Rating: N/A

Play it on: Android, iOS

Niantic's latest AR title adds a magical layer over our boring old muggle world. Using your mobile device, you can tap into this exciting fantasy, casting spells, battling monsters, and concocting potions.

One of the biggest differences between Wizards Unite and other AR games is its emphasis on a story. It might not be up to the standards of J.K. Rowling's major works, but it's an engaging reason to keep playing, and it provides some context as to why you're wandering around and visiting make-believe greenhouses and other points of interest.

Jurassic World Alive

ESRB Rating: N/A

Play it on: Android, iOS

If you wish that dinosaurs were still around, Ludia Inc.'s game may make you reconsider. In Jurassic Park Alive, dinosaurs are back and bigger than ever – well, at least they are if you look at your smartphone's screen. Seeing these titans come to life, superimposed over the world around you is impressive and practically worth the price of admission.

Once the novelty of seeing a T-rex in your backyard wears off, there's still plenty to do. As an amateur researcher, your job is to track down DNA fragments and combine (and evolve) them to bring new dinos to life. It has less of a competitive focus than some other AR games, but that doesn't mean it's a peaceful experience. These ancient beasts love to tussle, and you can pit your creatures against each other to see who truly is the king of the monsters.

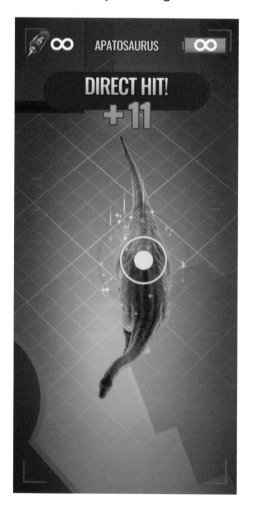

If Minecraft Dungeons Is Your Thing, Try...

Battle Chasers: Nightwar

ESRB Rating: T

Play it on: PC, PlayStation 4, Xbox One

The turn-based combat in Battle Chasers is more methodical than the faster action that most dungeon-crawlers provide, but it's no less engaging. It's not just about the battles, though. Airship Games takes the "dungeon" part of the genre seriously, serving up a deviously designed set of locations for your group of heroes to explore.

Battle Chasers is based on the comic from the '90s, but you don't need to be super familiar with it to enjoy the game. All you need to know is that these guys are tough, upgradeable, and ready to unleash torrents of destruction at a moment's notice. The lovingly animated visuals are a bonus, too.

Enchantress

Bounty: Break A Few Eggs
Complete The Break A Few Eggs Event

746

L1   X   □   △   ○   R1   R2

Diablo III

ESRB Rating: M

Play it on: PC, PlayStation 4, Switch, Xbox One

Diablo is the granddaddy of the dungeon-crawling genre, establishing the template that Minecraft Dungeons borrowed from. You like loot, combat, and finding loads of cool new items? Diablo III has all of that and more. Blizzard's game features several distinct classes to choose from, with plenty of different variations that allow you to play the way you like. Want to smash faces with a barbarian? Would you prefer to hang back and fire arrows as a demon hunter?

There's really something for everyone here, provided you want to knock evil back to the depths from which it came.

A word of caution: This one can get pretty gross, so if you're sensitive to blood and guts or live with people who are, you might want to steer clear of Diablo III.

Path of Exile

ESRB Rating: M

Play it on: PC, PlayStation 4, Xbox One

Minecraft Dungeons has some surprisingly deep item customization, but it can't compete with Path of Exile when it comes to player expression. There are millions of different ways to create your own unique character build, even before you factor in the dizzying size of its weapon and armor inventory. In short, if you enjoy complexity in your dungeon-crawling adventures, this is a safe bet.

Unlike most of the games on this list, you can check out Path of Exile without spending a dime. It's a free-to-play game, and generously so; you can play through the entirety of the campaign without paying, and the vast majority of the items that are for sale are just there to make your character look cool. As with Diablo III, Path of Exile contains some fairly strong stuff. Keep that in mind before you download it.

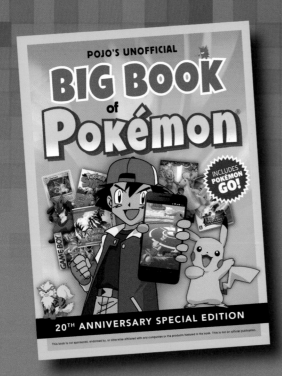

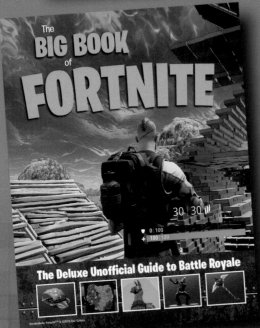